First Person Queer

First Person Queer

Who we are (so far)

edited by Richard Labonté and Lawrence Schimel

ARSENAL PULP PRESS
VANCOUVER

ARSENAL PULP PRESS
Suite 200, 341 Water Street
Vancouver, BC
Canada V6B 1B8
arsenalpulp.com

The publisher gratefully acknowledges the support of the Canada Council
for the Arts and the British Columbia Arts Council for its publishing
program, and the Government of Canada through the Book Publishing
Industry Development Program and the Government of British Columbia
through the Book Publishing Tax Credit Program for its publishing activities.

Text and cover design by Shyla Seller
Cover photograph © JupiterImages, *comstock.com*

Printed and bound in Canada

Library and Archives Canada Cataloguing in Publication

First person queer : who we are (so far) / edited by Richard Labonté
and Lawrence Schimel.

ISBN 978-1-55152-227-2

1. Homosexuality. 2. Bisexuality. 3. Transsexualism. 4. Gays—
Biography. 5. Bisexuals—Biography. 6. Transsexuals—Biography.
I. Labonté, Richard, 1949- II. Schimel, Lawrence

HQ75.15.F47 2007   306.76'6   C2007-904475-1

Contents

INTRODUCTION

We're All in Here, Somewhere

Richard Labonté & Lawrence Schimel

The call for submissions for this collection of first-person narratives was specifically non-specific: we weren't seeking merely memoir, though life stories were a part of what we wanted; we weren't seeking dogmatic queer theory, though challenging analysis was anticipated; and we weren't seeking just coming-out accounts, though the "click" of self-awareness suffuses many of the submissions—as it should, since what each contributor has in common with the others is the satisfaction of a realized sexual self.

While this anthology starts with our contributors sharing their individual, intimate stories, it is grounded in the concept of a collective identity—in the reality of a polymorphous, multidimensional, self-exploratory, celebratory, and sometimes even fractious community—and the relationship each of us has with its diverse herstories, hirstories, histories—with its stories. We can't claim that the grouping of voices we've selected is definitive—these are voices from the community, but they are not *the* voice of the community. At the same time, we wanted as inclusive a representation across the gender and chronological spectrum as possible.

And we got what we wanted: wisdom and introspection and sorrow, wit and passion and intimacy. There's welcome diversity, too—and not just among the self-definition markers (lesbian, bisexual, gay, transsexual, queer, ambivalent, questioning, none of the above, all of the above, exultantly genderqueer) of the contributors.

There is a healthy diversity of cultural disagreements and differing perceptions:

Joy Parks doesn't want any of her queer peers to wed; Daniel Gawthrop is one queer who is happy to be married. Andy Quan finds more pleasure in his garden than at one more damn Mardi Gras, already; Sky Gilbert hopes to be a gay old man who never gardens. Bonnie J. Morris revels in her proud dyke life; Chong-suk Han shuns being defined solely by his homosexuality. Jeffrey Rotin is very old-school when it comes to online cruising; Mette Bach cruises Myspace for new women to "friend." Being queer is easy for R. Gay; Nalo Hopkinson really does want a write-in option for "sexual orientation." Karen Taylor fuses her lesbian S&M energy with an adherence to Judaism; David Hatfield Sparks finds that fundamentalist zealots stole his daughter's affection.

And we have a splendid diversity of shared experiences:

Jane Van Ingen, hearing impaired, Gregory Woods, after prostate surgery, and Sandra Lambert, bearing scars, have relearned how to inhabit their bodies. Shawn Syms and Christopher DiRaddo have become comfortable with their respective hefty and hairy gay boy bodies, while sharon bridgforth exults in the mannish womanhood of her physique. Transgender elders Kate Bornstein and Gayle Roberts have negotiated the transition from a body that once was seen as "man" and now is lived as "woman," while young 'un S. Bear Bergman went in the opposite direction; all three meet in a settled middle ground.

And to illustrate the wondrous diversity of how words and ideas matter:

Joshua Dalton, still in his teens, Arden Eli Hill, in his twenties, and D. Travers Scott, midway through his thirties, write about how they have coped with the hate-filled epithets of intolerance hurled at them. Katherine V. Forrest, lesbian author, Tim Miller, gay performance artist, and Mary M. Davies, queer femme wordsmith, chart their queer lives through the words they write and the words they perform. Josh Kilmer-Purcell and Jason Timermanis acquire wisdom from the lives of the old aunties and queer ducks and gay heroes who are their forebears. Therese Szymanski liberates herself from constrictive labels like nerd and geek by finding others like herself.

There is also a delicious mélange of sexual experiences:

Stan Persky reflects on his sexual initiation, decades ago, as a horny sailor; Blaine Marchand also remembers his sexual initiation, also decades ago, with other eight-year-olds, and, at twelve, with the family priest. Simon Sheppard recalls the sexual haunts of San Francisco that link his past to his present; Achy Obejas comes upon correspondence that conjures up lost passion; and Robin Metcalfe's lust for classic chairs stirs up memories of young passion. Kirk Read is a fierce hooker when the door is slammed in his face, and David C. Findlay cherishes sex in public places. More exotically, as well as erotically, Stacey May Fowles tells why she's content to be the straight girl at the gay party, and George K. Ilsley weaves a fable about birds and sex.

And to complete the collection, Ivan E. Coyote, in "The Future of Francis," finds a hint of who we all have been, are, and will be, in the spirit of her young nephew.

No book exists in a vacuum, nor does a community. And just as our personal histories inform our present, our collective histories likewise have shaped and continue to shape us. We learn about our past, our traditions, through the stories we share with one another, no matter how we choose to tell each tale: spoken, written, in images, etc. It is crucial for us all to craft documents of our lives, both as individuals and as communities; it's our hope that *First Person Queer* serves as one such cultural document: a panoramic snapshot of queerdom today.

This anthology of first-person experiences can't possibly encompass all of us, but it contains many stories in each story, myriad lives reflected in every life. We're all in here, somewhere....

The Straight Girl at the Party

Stacey May Fowles

One irresponsible weeknight in Toronto, I had the rare pleasure of drinking too many pitchers of beer with a small group of female independent magazine professionals much like myself. Some I knew well and some of them I had just met that evening, each one standing behind a respected, progressive independent publication, each one coming from an ideology of open-minded politics and activist principles.

We started to play the inevitable "degrees of separation" game, a common practice in the Toronto independent media community, where the music, literary, and art scenes overlap and twist around each other in a way that inevitably means everyone has likely gotten naked with everyone else.

I soon learned that one of the women I had befriended that evening was familiar with my current live-in partner, that she had worked with him in a past life and had fond memories of him (both in personality and appearance—he was a "hottie," she hiccupped).

And then she said, "But you do know he's gay, don't you?"

She looked at me intently through her half-full pint glass, genuinely concerned and cautious, her hand touching mine. It was as if she had just told me a secret that had the potential to unravel my entire neat and tidy domestic world.

I laughed her off. "Well, he identifies as queer."

"Seriously, he had a boyfriend when I knew him. He's gay."

"He's queer."

"But he had a boyfriend. Maybe we're talking about a different person."

It was as if we were speaking different languages, throwing foreign lexicon at each other while emptying our glasses. This progressive media professional failed to successfully wrap her mind around the notion that someone I was sleeping with could also be the same person she knew who had a boy on his arm at various art events. She couldn't successfully reconcile the word queer with my claim of a heterosexual union with him, a fact that I'd like to blame on her beer intake.

But really, who can blame her at all?

Here comes the confession. This was not the first time I'd gotten the "You do know that he's gay?" question from a well-intentioned drinking companion, either about this particular partner or any of those who came before him. "I thought he was gay" is a common reaction when I announce an object of affection to friends, whether the crush started on a Saturday night at a dinner party or was founded in innocent pop-culture fiction (George Michael at age twelve, Stephen Patrick Morrissey at age seventeen, and more recently Toronto's Gentleman Reg at twenty-seven).

It's a wonder I've ever gotten laid.

If you go purely by the numbers, I am an experienced professional when it comes to procuring dead-in-the-water, poorly-thought-out sexual attractions: at last count I've experienced eight heart-thumping, swooning, silly-girl crushes on eight gay, bi, or queer-identified men, and believe it or not I've actually been a bona fide (albeit occasionally vague, denied, drunken, or accidental) sexual partner of five of those. Men I've merely kissed in the past are apt to question their sexuality simply because we locked lips a single time. I've received email messages from past lovers that have stated, "I still like girls," as if just to reassure me (and themselves).

I am that notorious.

As for my current partner—the queer in question over post-work beers—early in our relationship, after we had too many shots of tequila at a Mexican restaurant, he mustered the courage to take me home with him and break out a comprehensive set of beautiful self-portraits of him dressed in drag. I was more than elated. Sometimes I unabashedly provoke him to tell me tales of his homosexual conquests. I relish his gayness to a perverse and perhaps exploitative degree, am proud that my partner identifies as queer, and actually feel more comfortable in my relationship because he does, despite the fact that so many of the "het set" harass me about that clichéd fear that he'll leave me for what it is he's not getting. Regardless of whether the one I love leaves me for a man or a woman, the result is the same: I am left, and for someone who has had the ability to explore sexuality in a queer-positive setting, the leaving will likely have little to do with the parts I was or wasn't born with.

Besides, I argue that nowadays what he's not getting can easily be bought in a store and strapped on, which only seems to concern (and, well, disturb) the heteros that much more.

That old fag hag label is a worn-out one, but I suppose that it is at times a reasonable way to describe me, barring the fact that it is rare that a quintessential hag gets down and dirty with her gay male companions beyond the sexual parody of sweaty dance floor groping to the latest Madonna remix. Over the years I've developed quite a reputation for loving (and fucking) men who love men, and if sexuality is purely based on who you sleep with, then I am more than proud to identify as a gay man.

Of course we know that sexual preference cannot easily be defined by sexual practice (if only because those gay men that did share a lustful moment or two with me are not suddenly walking around calling themselves straight or bisexual as a result) and I am no longer willing to accept the psychological rationale that I seek to bed gay men because I am fulfilling a mental compulsion where I need to feel "safe," or because I am pursuing them because I need a "challenge." I also refuse to entertain the light-hearted critique that my intense attraction to gay male and queer culture is an offshoot of the fact that I'm looking to fail because "I'm not ready for a relationship." Instead, I've started to accept the fact that I love and feel comfortable with gay and queer-identified men because—wait for it—I am queer myself, and I tout the burgeoning theory of sexual fluidity as my rationale. I suppose I'm finally accepting the notion that there can indeed be straight queers and that it's more than okay for me to define myself as one.

We (and yes, I'm including myself—shock! horror!) have worked hard to develop a queer identity that lives outside of merely who we go to bed with; so why can't I, a heterosexual who feels most at home in queer culture, adopt it as a result?

Oh no, you say, here she comes, the straight girl at the party, the sexual identity tourist co-opting queer politics because it's convenient and easy for her to do so. Or maybe instead you're laughing at me because I'm simply rationalizing my seemingly endless and numerous attractions to men who have a preference for the parts I don't have? Do I even have the authority to suggest that queer identity can be adopted by heterosexuals, and thus cure how lost they feel in heterosexual culture? Is that where queer is going? I'll accept the subsequent reactions as valid, but in the reality that is my daily life, queer and gay culture is where I fit the best.

Which is not to say that I fit in all that comfortably all the time. I proudly adhered a "Queer" sticker to my chest at the 2005 Toronto Pride Parade, only to have a close friend tell me that I wasn't allowed to wear it.

So a sticker that stated I was "Str8" replaced it.

Although I am primarily heterosexual by some pre-determined definitions, I've never been comfortable with or in hetero culture in general. And I'm coming to believe that it can be just as offensive for someone to belittle my less than mainstream desires as some sort of mental defect as it is to subscribe to the horrible hetero-sexist assumption that homosexuals experience a similar mental defect. And as a result, I'd much rather live and fuck in a (queer) culture that occasionally giggles at my naïveté and my continued crush on George Michael, which questions and critiques the convenience of my co-opted identity, than suffer in a mainstream culture that seeks to stifle and offend me.

I certainly don't want to subscribe to a culture that constantly questions who I love and doubts if they love me back. In fact, I refuse to be a part of that line of questioning at all, no matter how many beers have been had when it's brought up.

I'm much happier being the straight girl at the party.

Uncle Arthur

Josh Kilmer-Purcell

Uncle Arthur sits across from me in the garden, picking bits of stray cigarette tobacco from his cardigan. The cardigan is likely thirty years old, at least. But it looks brand new. Arthur (or Little Chicken, as the Provençal villagers have inexplicably, yet endearingly, nicknamed him) is always impeccably dressed.

This is twelve years ago. I'm in my mid-twenties, and he is nearly seventy-two. I've just wrapped up tearfully telling him the story of how my latest boyfriend had dumped me while we were vacationing at his Swedish ancestral home somewhere way the fuck up in the Arctic Circle. My vacation shattered, and my ticket back to New York not valid for another week, I'd trained and planed my way to Massanne, France, to Arthur's tiny backyard garden.

"Well," he says, still picking at the fallen tobacco, not bothering to look at my tear-stained face, "that all sounds terribly normal."

He finally looks up, showing a sudden interest. "But you've arrived at a good time. *The asparagus has come to market!*"

And for reasons he's taught me, over and over to this day, I suddenly realized that it all *was* terribly normal. And that asparagus would be lovely for lunch.

I met my uncle once when I was five, and then not again until I was twenty-one, but not due to any malice on the part of my other relatives. It was just that since World War II, Arthur had spent his summers in Geneva and his winters in Provence with his partner, Bob. Wisconsin was a long way from France. There was very little reason for either of us to traverse the globe for each other.

Until the day—my final year of college—when I realized that my own particular brand of young adult angst had a name.

Gay.

Then the early memory of a lithe, strawberry blond, goateed man with a walking stick and exotic presents came back to me.

I had a gay uncle.

Two gay uncles, I soon found out, after my mother informed me of Bob.

I was a fledgling drama queen, and the first time I flew over to visit them, I realized that I'd found my genetic roots in Arthur.

Arthur was an old-school poofter, the "woman in the relationship." As derogatory as that sounds to today's modern faggotry, it suited Arthur well. And I don't think he'd particularly mind the designation. Throughout his fifty-plus years with the Orson Wellesian Bob, he kept the two of them on a social schedule that rivaled royalty. Sometimes literally. Bob and Arthur were the token "boys" of their ex-pat set, and as such, they'd been to soirées with Princess Grace; dinners with innumerous artists, writers, and actors; and on cruises with society mavens of all nationalities.

They were equally well known for hosting their own raucous parties. During one, the most popular French New Wave actress of the day (Françoise Fabian from *My Night at Maud's)* was chased across the moonlit Provençal yard by a goose, which was followed by Bob, who was shooting a shotgun in the vague vicinity of the angry fowl—as well as Françoise and the rest of the drunken, laughing partygoers. Miraculously all the guests survived. And the bird was served at the next night's party.

Arthur sat quietly—dutifully—throughout the years watching Bob's larger-than-life antics. He sighed on the sidelines with deceptive dispassion, *tsk*-ing softly to himself and picking fallen tobacco bits from his sweater.

Thus it was hard to impress him with my own youthful petty dramas.

Which was exactly what a budding drama queen like me needed to witness at my young age. Perspective. Not as a lesson on how to keep things grounded in reality; the opposite, actually. It taught me that I really had to ramp up the traumas in my life if I wanted to be taken seriously.

I credit my present seven-year relationship to Little Chicken and Bob. I find it difficult to imagine how gay men can couple up without having older same-sex role models. I'm loathe to witness young gay men emulating their parents' heterosexual relationship. Like Arthur, I sigh off to the side, waiting for the young homo relationship to disintegrate simply because they don't know how to patch the leaks.

A few years after the Swedish trifle, I was visiting Arthur and Bob around Christmastime when they received a holiday card that included a photo. The man in the shot looked to be about their age, and decidedly French. He was dressed neatly in a slightly dated but still fabulous outfit, not unlike the type I'd seen Arthur wear on evenings out.

"Who's this?" I asked, holding up the photo during a lunch of hearty leftover cassoulet cooked by Bob for a small dinner party the previous evening.

"That's Jean Paul," Arthur answered.

"How is he?" Bob gruffed, looking away from the television for the first time during the meal. He would watch *Columbo* reruns at lunch every day, to the overly dramatic disgust of Arthur.

Arthur put on his unwittingly retro-trendy reading glasses, raised his nose slightly, and read the card to himself.

"He's fine," he concluded, without ever sharing a word of the message. He turned the card back over to examine the illustration on the cover. Sigh. "What an ex-*quis*-ite card."

Bob harrumphed in gravel-voiced assent without even glancing away from *Columbo*.

Later, in the kitchen, as Arthur and I loaded up the dishwasher, Arthur nudged me. I turned and he said: "You know about Jean Paul, eh?" Arthur tends to begin all questions as declarations, and end all declarations as questions. It's another professional drama queen trait I've picked up from him. It makes everything that comes out of one's mouth sound like a mysterious conspiracy.

"No," I answered, knowing that a long, delicious afternoon story would follow—accompanied by a bottomless glass of Pastis and old photo albums.

Over the course of the next three hours in the garden—safely out of Bob's earshot—Arthur explained that Jean Paul was the man for whom Bob had left Arthur, back in 1972.

One afternoon, Arthur had come home from a busy day at the World Bank in Geneva to find Bob missing. A phone call later confirmed that Bob had fled to Paris with Jean Paul, who they'd both met at a party a few weeks earlier. Arthur promptly went on a bender with such a histrionic flair that it crossed six European borders and ended in a sanatorium.

But beyond the obvious tutorial this story served up to my inner drama queen, there was another, larger lesson I was learning.

Bob stayed with Jean Paul until early 1975, nearly three years.

He eventually came "home." But unlike a heterosexual couple (who likely would have divorced immediately anyway) those three years didn't become a distant secret, never to be spoken of again.

In fact, Jean Paul remained a close friend of both Bob and Arthur.

The phrase "close friend," when uttered by Arthur and followed by "*eh?*" probably meant exactly what I thought it did. But that wasn't the important part of the story—or all the hundreds of other stories my fey uncle has told me over the years.

What was important, I learned, was that gay men's relationships are different than straight couples'. They are *supposed* to be. And because there are so few of us lucky enough to have an Uncle Arthur and Uncle Bob as family pioneers, most gay couples are given the task—and the freedom—to figure out our own unique solutions to our largely self-inflicted dramas.

For gay men planning on spending the next fifty years together, everything *should* be terribly normal. Our very own terrible, awful, wonderful, abnormal normal.

And if that means spending from 1972 to 1975 without your partner—that's okay.

It will add another ex-*quis*-ite Christmas card to your life's collection.

Genderquerulous

Nalo Hopkinson

I recently received a notice about an online questionnaire gathering information for a book on women's sexual fantasies. I clicked on the link.

The first question was, "What is your relationship/lifestyle status?" It invited respondents to tick off as many of the following categories that applied to them: Live-in relationships/marriages; steady/long-term relationships (not live-in); children; no children; single and very sexually active/playing the field; single and moderately sexually active; single and occasionally sexually active; celibate by choice or circumstance; virgin. There was no space for a write-in answer. So if I was sexually active, I could be single and dating, or I could have steady relationships. I couldn't have steady relationships and also be dating.

The second question was, "What is your sexual orientation?" It gave three possible responses; "heterosexual," "bisexual," and "homosexual." Again, there was no space for a write-in answer, although other questions on the questionnaire did give that option.

I prefer to say "queer," but I could have checked off "bisexual." It would have been close enough. Yet when it came to the first question, no matter how many boxes I were to tick off, the answer would have been a lie. The right answer, even though it reflects not just my experience, but that of many women, simply wasn't an option.

The author and I have a passing acquaintance, so I wrote to ask her whether she would consider adding a write-in box to those two first questions. Her friendly reply said that she wouldn't do so because I could write in the other write-in boxes on the questionnaire.

She urged me to write whatever I wished, and to have fun with it.

The author was quite right; I could have wedged my experience into places on the questionnaire where that information was not explicitly being requested. I did not. I did not respond to the questionnaire at all. Sometimes it's nice to be recognized and included upfront, rather than having to elbow out room for oneself yet again.

A couple of years ago, I was invited to be a guest author at a university conference in the US on black queer sexuality. I don't recall whether the conference organizers said it in so many words, but I'd guess that a large part of the reason they'd invited me was because I was a queer, black author. It sounded like a great conference, and a bold one for them to undertake. I accepted their invitation. Then I sat down and did some thinking.

I was forty-four years old. I'd been a published fiction writer for seven years. I was used to being in front of audiences, but the conference would be one of my first public appearances as a queer, poly woman. Definite *gulp* moment for a formerly straight, monogamous, nice middle-class Caribbean girl; and one of many gulp moments I've had over the past five years. Doubtless there are many more to come. Moments like writing this piece, for instance. I have none of the comfort my out, queer friends and lovers have gained from years of experience, and since my writing career gives me visibility, I am working my stuff out in public. Coming to consciousness as a woman, a feminist, and black had been many doddles by comparison.

I tried to figure out what, if anything, my participation might add to the conference. I thought about my still very shaky queer self-definition, and why it was shaky. Hell, it even felt like a problem that it *was* shaky. How often had I heard, "*Ever since I was a child, I knew I was attracted to people of my gender*"? How often had I heard people defending same-sex desire with the argument, "*We/ they can't help it; we/they are just born this way*"? I was supposed to be possessed of some kind of innate, "natural" queerness that had been there as long as I could remember. I was supposed to have had secret longings for other women.

I wasn't, and I hadn't. And yet, that is both true and false. In this, as in so much else in my life, I'm apparently unnatural. As a teen, I'd had the very common experience of a schoolgirl crush on a stylish female teacher, but as powerful as it was, it was more about envying her self-confidence and her fashion sense than about anything explicitly sexual. Like the time a few years ago when I found myself taking a trans friend home for the night, I tend to act first through a trepidation that gongs so loudly that I have a hard time hearing whether it's masking any desire. I figure out the desire part in the moment or later, if at all. Form following function. Identity following action. Or something like that, only messier. If the popular narrative of knowing one's sexuality before experiencing it is the only way to be, I don't have an orientation. I have a dis-orientation.

The short answer, which, for expediency's sake, uses commonly accepted words, assumes that those words mean what we think they mean, and that we share the same interpretation of their meanings. *Then*: I was attracted to men. I was straight. *And now*: I am attracted to women and men. I am bisexual.

The long answer, which uses words and concepts that some askers will not understand, or will consider false, trendy, or irrelevant: *None, some, and/or all of the above.* Or, "Yes, but...."

At some point in my early teens, my parents gave me a book about sex. That would have been in the early 1970s, I think. I already knew much of the information it contained. There was one tidbit of new information, a brief paragraph on sexual orientation. It basically said that there were three types: homosexual, heterosexual, and bisexual.

I'd vaguely known that people were straight or gay, but that may have been the first time that I came across the information that one could like both women and men. That there were more possibilities for me beyond the unexamined trajectory of grow up, get married to a man, get pregnant, and spend the rest of my lifetime accommodating to being yoked in connubial ... bliss? From what I was seeing around me, it didn't look that blissful for most people. But I was still young, and that ironclad future seemed quite a thankful distance away.

Yeah, maybe I was dense, but to me, sexual orientation was something that adults had. That was the first time in my young life that it occurred to me to wonder what my own sexual orientation was: attracted to men? To women? Some degree of both? I knew, or thought I knew, what women were. They had breasts and vaginas and wore dresses and makeup and high heels. They did housework and gave birth to and looked after babies, sometimes with help from their husbands. Women were supposed to be weaker and dumber than men, though my parents blessedly weren't committed to reinforcing that particular stereotype. When I asked myself whether I was attracted to women, I went by my understanding of the word "women." And the answer was no. I was on my way to being one, and that was mostly okay. But I didn't want to have sex with women.

However, I kind of liked the idea of being bisexual. It seemed to offer a range of possibilities, and that was exciting. Plus my mental map is such that whenever possible, I'll plump for *other*. At fewer than fifteen years of life, I could already discern that my world configured bisexual as other. But my impromptu and unscientific test had already registered a response of *no attraction to women*, so, a bit regretfully and a bit thankfully (for I also already knew that any kind of queer desire would be problematic, perhaps even dangerous), I let the notion of being bisexual go. I didn't, in any case, feel a strong pull toward it. It was more a notional thing, along the lines of, *Wouldn't it be neat if I could speak twenty-two languages fluently?*

Did I have a concept of what men were? Yes, probably. And when

I asked myself whether I was attracted to men, body and mind gave me a strong *yes* back. Men had started to smell good to me which, as one of the many signals that I was becoming something significantly different than my childhood sense of self was used to, I found both startling and intriguing.

So that was that, I figured. I was straight.

But there was a problem with that. I had already taken in the warnings that it was dire and dangerous to have any same-sex desire. I was on my way to adulthood, but I was still a child, and a girl child at that. I was very much aware of being vulnerable to violence, and very afraid of it. And I was, as much as possible, an extremely obedient child. (My parents might have begged to differ, but I was.) How, given that level of deterrence, does anyone manage to figure out what their true pattern of desire is? We are social beings. Desire doesn't operate in a vacuum. Our need to be loved by others, sexually and otherwise, can't help but affect the ways in which we desire.

I've already hinted at the other problem; most of the dominant mainstreams of our world will only admit to one construction of gender—an inseparable conflation of "penis = male = masculine" and "breasts/vagina = female = feminine." Those mainstreams insist that you like "women (feminine)" or "men (masculine)." A few of them allow for the possibility of liking both, though they cast it as a suspect state of affairs best avoided or outgrown. Apparently, bisexual people are either in denial or non-existent; certainly, we are untrustworthy. Apparently, normal people are gay or straight, and it's a permanent orientation. We're "born that way." Given those rigid, binary constructions of sexuality and gender, the best way I could map my attraction to them was "straight." It was the one to which my body responded the most unequivocally with something I could recognize as desire. It didn't even occur to me that it was a poor fit.

It's difficult for me to explain nowadays, because there was other evidence. I came across the occasional person who didn't fit the binary. I silently cheered many of them on. When Annie Lennox appeared on an awards show in Elvis drag, I was riveted to the television. *The Rocky Horror Picture Show* and the very bent *Cabaret* were among my favorite films. But I didn't think of that kind of fascination as being reflective of sexual attraction.

Fast-forward to my late thirties when, after a mostly disastrous and lonely love life, I hooked up with the lovely man who is currently a life partner of mine. (I no longer do monogamy, so having more than one partner at the same time is possible.) My partner is a political human; queer, black, poly, feminist, sex-positive, and loud about it all. And smart, and caring, and curious; did I mention curious? He kept poking at the holes he perceived in my self-definition until he realized how much he was upsetting me. But he wasn't the only one asking questions. I was, too.

When the film *The Adventures of Priscilla, Queen of the Desert* came to town, I was intrigued by the character of the formerly straight gay man who had a wife and child he loved and who loved him. I loved the character of the transwoman who hadn't forgotten how to throw a punch. I loved the scene of the Aboriginal people and the white drag queens and tranny partying in the outback. (The caricature of the highly dramatic, bitchy Asian prostitute who spat Bali H'ai English from one end and tennis balls from the other was another matter entirely, but I won't get into that now.) But the character who struck me the strongest was that of Bob, the mechanic. A nondescript, nearly invisible man of no perceptible "difference." Yet he dates a prostitute, then woos a transwoman. What was he? How does one define the apparent insider who's drawn to outsiders? To go by what we saw in the film, he was straight. But straight with a difference. I asked a few people. Some didn't know why I thought it was significant. Some thought I was just being arch. No one gave me an answer that satisfied my questions.

It took me until my forties to start to figure this all out. At that time, I began a painful process of coming out to myself as—what? "The love that has no goddamned name," I once joked through tears. I decided I needed a T-shirt that read, "100% Kinsey-what-the-fuck." Some of you are probably rolling your eyes, but it felt like a serious dilemma to me. For a couple of years, I didn't feel any reliable attraction to anyone but said partner.

I finally began to come up with answers, wonderful, scary answers. I'm not easily attracted to straight men (those born with penises attached, that is), or to straight women, or to people who are exclusively vanilla, or monogamous, or to femmes (those born with female genitalia, that is). But you know what? That leaves *everyone else*: genderqueers, queer/bi men, butches, bois, nellies, trannyfags, you name it. And that's without getting into feminism, or politics, or whether you pull your socks up or roll them down when you're wearing shorts. My mistake had been falling into the conceptual trap that the definitions of "man" and "woman" I'd been fed were all there was. Duh. What I'd needed were more adjectives!

I decided that I would attend the conference on black queer sexuality as the spokesperson for *I don't know shit*. In fact, that's exactly what I did. I saw enough sighs of relief and shoulders relaxing to know that I was reflecting the experience of at least some of the other people in attendance.

It's still disorienting. It's still scary. And my mother's afraid for my reputation. (She needn't be. Near as I can tell, it's improved.) I still don't have a short answer, or a single answer, or a definite answer that works for every situation and every case or that is the same answer I had yesterday. I was once interviewed by a lesbian magazine. When asked my sexual orientation, I playfully responded, "trannychaser." They refused to print my answer. They probably did me a favor. But I'm enjoying my life more than I ever have before. I'm meeting more and more people who navigate the same territory. I'm learning from their examples. I'm getting used to asking for "other" write-in boxes on questionnaires (though I rarely get them).

A Never-Gardening Gay Old Man

Sky Gilbert

"I grow old … I grow old … I shall wear the bottoms of my trousers rolled," says T.S. Eliot. And it's hard, when you're a gay man, to escape all the prescriptions for what you should be. When I was a little boy I was mortally afraid, everyday, that I might be gay (I was generally a frightened child). But it was not simply gayness itself—in fact I had no clear imagining of the act, or for that matter what sex itself was. But I had a very clear picture then, in my mind, of the aging homosexual—lonely, at a single table, in a dingy flat, gazing hopelessly at a candle—utterly, relentlessly solitary, and desperately sad. I didn't want to be *that*, I would tell myself over and over, please, anything else but that.

I am fifty-four years old—but I profess to forty-five at parties, because I still get some *oooh*-ing and *ahh*-ing when I eventually tell people my real age. This proves that I have age *issues*. Of course, we all do. If we're gay, how could we not? In Ian Young's marvelous book, *The Stonewall Experiment*, he theorizes that AIDS is not only a physical disease, but a mental one. After coming out so gloriously in the 1970s, many of us died in the 80s—perhaps in part because we couldn't imagine what it would be like to be gay and grow old; gay culture gave us no picture at all of how we might grow up. The images we could imagine of being gay and old were just too, too scary. So scary, in fact, that an almost morbidly hedonistic, self-destructive life became normal. Some of us still seem to dread a long life. I think about crystal meth, I think about gleeful, recreational unsafe sex, and wonder, could these behaviors be about that dread?

Of course it's solipsistic and a little selfish to think we own suicide;

human beings in general are suicidal, or else no one would ever smoke, drink, or go rock-climbing. But even if you violently disagree with the notion that gay culture tends to be suicidal, surely you must agree that there are precious few role models out there for happy, aging gay men. Rent a gay movie, and you are sure to find that the leading roles are played by two very young hunky guys. Most often, one character is blond and the other is dark, and the light-haired one is pretty, and has left sex behind, so to speak (because of AIDS). But the darker, more muscled character convinces the blond to take it up the bum (with a condom, of course). Inevitably, in these tedious flicks, there will also be a friend and movie-going companion—typically the Older Gay Man. The Older Gay Man is often effeminate (older gay men are effeminate in these movies, whereas younger gay men have somehow miraculously moved beyond that stereotype). And the Older Gay Man will be one of two types, the villain—who I call the Dirty Old Gay Man—or the lovely endearing fart (who I call the Ever-Gardening Old Gay Man).

These are the roles offered to us by movies and, I would posit, by our culture in general. The dichotomy is important; we cannot choose whether or not to grow old but we can choose what kind of older gay man to be. To be sexual and old, society tells us, is a bad thing. If we are non-sexual and old, there is, as Barbra Streisand reminds us, certainly a place for us. Nobody likes a dirty old man. And older men, gay or straight, should (everyone thinks) focus themselves on the proper pursuits of the old: crossword puzzles, mystery novels, light housekeeping, the dispensation of words of wisdom, and gardening (if the ol' back is up to it, of course!). Salt and pepper hair, a paunch, and wearing spectacles low on the nose always help a little bit with the image.

I am trying to buck this trend. I comfort myself with the fact that though I have age *issues*, I do not dress inappropriately for my age, or at least not as inappropriately as some. I have left the tank tops and the spandex behind, and the form-fitting, wet-look, heavily patterned shirts, as well as shiny fabrics of any ilk. I have not been able to say goodbye to the odd string-net T-shirt, which yes, I let peek through from underneath a sweatshirt top. Okay, not peek—I actually do still go out to bars and show my cleavage. Oh yes, and what the hell, I do still get drunk and work myself up into the kind of uninhibited state of free association which I associate with fuck time. Then it's off to the baths.

I go there at least twice a week.

I know, this is unforgivable behavior for a fifty-four year old. But remember, I came out of the closet when I was nearly thirty. During my thirties I was drunk/stoned/poppered out of my mind, and quite literally royally fucked, every night of the week. So two nights a week of some booze and sex is actually, in my case, elderly moderation. Do I still get laid? Most of the time. Do I settle—that is, have I given up on my sexual fantasies? Well my sexual fantasies are pretty and twenty-eight years old, and though they don't walk through my doorway every week, they do come by enough to keep me coming, and coming back. Some, to my chagrin, seem to especially like an older man. They are frighteningly hungry for me, and even objectify me. It's Daddy they want, and they can't get enough of him.

I also have a lover who is thirty-seven years old, and we occasionally have sex. But sex is not what our relationship is about. Sex was never what it was about. He is deeply beautiful—that is beautiful and deep—and kind, and slightly insane, and infuriating. He challenges me and makes me laugh, and he is my romantic partner, and my soulmate.

I also have friends, old friends—most of them I have known for nearly twenty years now, and that means that we have lots of memories to share, and we are growing old together (though most of them are about ten years younger than I am). I have tried to make friends with men my own age, but most of them have decided to garden and wear spectacles, or to haunt the baths and darkrooms—but with self-loathing and desperation, wailing about how difficult it is to find a lover. (I want to ask those who are so desperate for a lover two things: Do you love yourself? Are you capable or desirous of actually loving someone else? It takes a lot of time and energy to love somebody. You might be better off without the trouble!)

Of course all these things could disappear. My boyfriend and I have our ups and downs (though we celebrated our eighth anniversary last September—which is fifty in gay years!). Not only could that disappear, but my health could go, at any moment. Or the boys could stop coming around at the bathhouse.

Or I could die, sooner than later.

But this is the threat that we all are under; life is fragile and things change. I have not found it particularly lonely to be an aging homosexual. What I do find lonely is being a writer; because my work is conceived and executed in solitude, and the subjects I write about are often unpleasant—and thus difficult to share with others (hence the low sales of my novels). I recently started meditating. I found that—when kick comes to shove—I am my own best friend. I hope my lover doesn't disappear, and that the boys at the baths don't stop coming around, and that the old friends still want to have a drink. But if they all go away, I still have me.

And when I go back to that picture I had in my head as a child of the aging, lonely homosexual, I see now that what was missing at the other side of the table wasn't another person. It may very well have been another version of myself—smiling, accepting, and loving—loving *me*.

As no one else can, actually.

Hoowahyoo?

Kate Bornstein

"Who are you?" asks the third blue-haired lady, peering up at me through the thick lenses of her rhinestone cat eye glasses. Only it comes out in one word, like "Hoowahyoo?" I'm wearing black, we all are. It's my mother's funeral service after all, and the little old ladies are taking inventory of the mourners. Me, I have to take inventory of my own identities whenever someone asks me who I am, and the answer that tumbles out of my mouth is rarely predictable. But this is my mother's funeral, and I am devastated, and to honor the memory of my mom, I'm telling each of them the who of me I know they can deal with.

"I'm Kate Bornstein," I answer her in my quiet-quiet voice. "Mildred's daughter."

"Daughter?!" She shoots back incredulously the same question each of her predecessors has asked, because everyone knew my mother had two sons. That was her claim to fame and prestige among this crowd. No do-nothing daughters in my mother's family, no sir. Two sons. That was her worth as a woman.

"Mildred never mentioned she had a daughter." The eyes behind those glasses are dissecting my face, looking for family resemblances. When I was a boy, I looked exactly like my father. Everyone used to say so. Then, when I went through my gender change, those same people would say, "Y' know, you look just like your mother." Except I'm tall.

Nearly six feet of me in mourning for the passing of my mother, and I'm confronting this brigade of matrons whose job it seems to be to protect my mother from unwanted visitors on this morning of her memorial service down the Jersey shore.

"You're her daughter? So who's your father? It's not Paul, am I right?"

Now there would be a piece of gossip these women could gnaw on over their next mahjongg game. "Mildred had another child," they'd say after calling two *bams*, "a daughter no less! And Paul, God rest his soul, he never knew."

My mother had told only a tight circle of friends about my gender change. She knew that spreading the word meant she'd be torn to shreds by the long pink fingernails so favored by the arbiters of propriety of the small town she lived in. She was raised in a nearly orthodox household. As a young girl, she would wake up every morning just in time to hear the men and boys wake up and utter the phrase, "Thank God I was not born a woman." She lived her life placing her self-worth on the presence of the men in her life. Her father, a successful merchant, died a year before I was born. Her husband, a successful doctor, died a year before I told her that one of her two sons was about to become a dyke. She preferred the word lesbian. "My son, the lesbian," she would tell her close friends, with a deep sigh and a smile on her lips.

My mother was there the night the rabbi asked me who I was. I was a senior in college, a real hippie: beard, beads, and suede knee-high moccasins with fringe hanging down past my calves. I was home for some holiday or other, and my parents thought it would be nice if I came to synagogue with them. They wanted to show off their son who was going to Brown. I'd always enjoyed Friday night services. There's something lullingly familiar about the chanting, something comforting in the old melodies and the Hebrew that I never ever understood although I had it down phonetically.

But when the rabbi gave his sermon, I was incensed. To this day, I don't remember what I was so outraged by, any sense of my anger having been eclipsed by the events that followed. But there I was, jumping to my feet in the middle of the rabbi's sermon, arguing some point about social justice.

My father was grinning. He'd never been bar mitzvah'ed, having kicked his rabbi in the shins the first day of Hebrew school. My mother had her hand over her mouth to keep from laughing. She was never very fond of our rabbi, not since the time he refused to make a house call to console my father the night my grandfather died. So there we were, the rabbi and the hippie, arguing rabbinical law and social responsibility. We both knew it was going nowhere. He dismissed me with a nod. I dismissed him with a chuckle, and the service continued. On the way out of the synagogue, we had to file by the rabbi, who was shaking everyone's hand.

"Albert," he said to me, peering up through what would later be known as John Lennon glasses, "Hoowahyoo? You've got the beard, so now you're Jesus Christ?"

I've done my time as an evangelist. Twelve years in the Church of Scientology, and later, when I'd escaped Hubbard's minions, four or five years as a reluctant spokesperson for the world's fledgling transgender movement. But somewhere in between Scientology and postmodern political activism, I found time to do phone sex work. My mother never knew about that part. It was one of the who's I'd become that I knew she couldn't deal with. So I never told her of the day I was standing in line in the corner store in West Philly, chatting with the woman behind the counter. From behind, a deep male voice said, "Excuse me, who are you?" And I turned to see this middle-aged yuppie peering up at me through tortoise-rimmed glasses.

"Stormy?" he asked me. Stormy was the name I'd chosen for the smoky-voiced phone sex grrrrl who was an erotic dancer on the side and had a tattoo on her thigh. "Stay on the line with me a little longer, sugar," I'd purr into the phone, "and I'll tell you what it is."

So this young urban professional was standing behind me looking like he'd died and was meeting the Virgin Mary. I tried to remember what fantasy of his we'd played out. But I was scared. Way scared. If word got out that Stormy was a tranny, I would lose my job for sure. I fixed this guy with the same icy stare I'd learned from my mother, and he eventually slunk away to inspect the Pringles.

My mother died before she could hear the blue-haired ladies ask "Hoowahyoo" of the tall-tall woman with mascara running down her cheeks. She never heard the producer from the *Ricki Lake Show* ask me, "Who are you?" when I told her I wasn't a man or a woman. My mother never heard the Philadelphia society matron ask me the same question when I attempted to attend her private, women-only AA group.

My mother only once asked me, "Who are you?" It was about a week before she died. "Hoowahyoo, Albert?" she asked anxiously, mixing up names and pronouns in the huge dose of morphine, "Who are you?" I told her the truth: I was her baby, I always would be. I told her I was her little boy, and the daughter she never had. I told her I loved her.

"Ha!" she exclaimed, satisfied with my proffered selection of who's. "That's good. I didn't want to lose any of you, ever."

Cool/Queer/Cool

R. Gay

There was no teenage angst or self-recrimination. There was no self-doubt, fear of damnation or concern for my mortal soul. I never had a problem accepting myself as queer. Being queer, in fact, was easy.

I realized, sometime in high school, between boyfriends and bemoaning just how uncool I really was, that I wanted to sleep with girls more than boys. A few years later, while wasting time in college, spending all of my time in the drama department surrounded by the "freaks" of our little school, I came out, without much fanfare at all. I started dating girls, and by dating I mean falling into bed before the first date and promising my eternal love within the first, say, seventy-two hours of a relationship. I experimented with unique hairdos and adorned myself with pride rings and some very frightening, I now realize, rainbow paraphernalia. I redecorated my car with rainbow flags and the ubiquitous symbol of the Human Rights Campaign. I was a lesbian, and I was letting the world know because I believed that one is not really a lesbian unless there are as many outward signs of her sexuality as possible. It was the 1990s. I was very invested in my here-ness, my queerness, my get-used-to-it-ness. I was ACT-ing UP.

There's something about being young and queer that was more about the pose of queerness than the actual living of the thing. It was all so seductive, knowing that I was different, knowing that I was part of a world to which not everyone could gain admittance. I was a hot mess. I can accept that about myself now. I essentially ruined the back of a perfectly good car with twenty different stickers declaring my pride and my sexuality and my avid interest in kink.

I was in the throes of late adolescence, where you crave visibility as much as you crave anonymity and the secrecy of subculture. What I remember about that time is not the relationships I had (disastrous) or the sex (quite excellent) but rather, how cool it felt to let the world know that I was something not the same.

As I got older, I became less interested in that sort of visibility. I became disillusioned with the idea of the queer community because that community and I, we were an awkward fit. There aren't a lot of roles in the community for a mouthy black girl as anything but the token hag or amusing and anecdotal Black Friend. I didn't go back in the closet. Rather, I chose to stop living my life as a statement because all the posturing and shucking and jiving felt hollow, unnecessary, disrespectful. And while I was less involved with the Community, I still felt like I was part of a community.

I've had more difficulty accepting myself as bisexual than I ever did accepting that I was a lesbian. It felt traitorous. A few years ago, I admitted to myself that I was still interested in men in more than a "Brad Pitt is slick hot sexy" kind of way. But I worried what my friends, exes, and the Community would think. I never even broached the subject with my parents. Because what bothered me the most was that people would think that being a lesbian had been a phase for me, when that was so very not the case. What I feared was that I would no longer be part of a community, that I might be seen with my boyfriend and not be recognized as something not the same.

For me, the real challenge of being queer is that you're always struggling with definitions and the borders of identity. Beyond the self-acceptance and the societal maxims and the homophobia and the excessive expressions of queer youth, there are a lot of people out there (I imagine, or is it I hope?) who struggle with understanding the meaning of who we are as queer and who struggle with the boundaries that seem to be constantly shifting. There are so many things going on in the queer world today that shock me and intrigue me and scare me. Every time I think I have a handle on the queer community and my place in it, a new brand of queer emerges.

It all makes me feel old, out of touch, square, when for so long, I've prided myself on being a fixture of various subcultures. As I was growing up in the world of queerness and kink, one of the key phrases was "Your Kink is Okay." It meant that I may not enjoy the same things you enjoy, but I wholeheartedly support your right to do what it is that you do. It was a gesture of *noblesse oblige*—though again, looking back, I can see that it was a little pretentious and full of awkward assumptions about people caring or needing to care about outside opinions of their lifestyles. I mention this because one of the things I've realized is that queerness evolves. The free-for-all attitudes I had in the late 1990s are not so much part of who I am today. Sometimes, I think, Your Kink is Not Okay, and I feel a twinge of guilt. Again, I feel like a traitor. But increasingly, for me, being queer is also about being okay with being different from the queer community as well as the straight community. Being queer is daring to hold unpopular opinions. Being queer is being unafraid to voice those unpopular opinions.

I sound like an elderly crone at the age of thirty-two, but it feels all too easy to be queer these days. I'm a hypocrite for saying that because it was likely too easy for me. In many ways, it's now cool to be queer. Maybe this makes me uncomfortable because for once, even out here on the fringes, I'm one of the cool kids.

a wo'mn called sir

sharon bridgforth

people often assume me to be a Black man   and i am
but mostly i'm a Black butch lesbian
which to me is about gender identity/in combination with
energy sensibility style and Spirit.

for me to claim myself butch was a process
in fact the first time someone called me butch/i was deeply insulted.
for years i'd been called tomboy mannish a stud and sir/none of
which was a bother
however
butches/in my mind
were white women who wanted to be men
and i ain't white
i've never wanted to be a man   and
i am not interested in engaging with women who want a woman to
    be a man.
so to be called butch   to me/was like being called an oreo.
i decided to work through my initial response to the word because
people kept using it as a label to refer to me. during the process of
working to understand why people saw me/called me butch
a lot of things surfaced   like
remembering being ten years old looking at the sears & roebuck's
catalogue over and over daydreaming about the outfits i wanted—
all those great color coordinated boys' shorts and tees that would
be mine one day/when i had money.

i realized that as an adult i dreamt about stylish men's clothes
i wanted to buy. and
it became clear that
in my mind
my body was a man's body.
not because i wanted to be a man
certainly not because i lacked woman curves
but/because i didn't see my body as
woman.
and i couldn't imagine women's clothes ever accurately expressing
how i felt/inside
           which has caused many a fashion crisis over the years.
my Black gurl hips and thighs don't look right in men's pants/my
big woman titties don't really work in men's shirts and even if i
considered women's clothes something to dream about—they
always felt too small too short and too confining. too womanish.
and the gregory hines que suave/Colored man sleek city *gq* look
that was my inside self was too phat for my wallet.

thinking about my butchness i realized that
women have rarely spoken to me in public bathrooms/in fact
they often rush out when they see me come in
while nervously trying to direct me to the men's bathroom
or openly curse my existence with cutting eyes and curt body language.
but once/in dallas texas while i washed my hands in a bathroom
at the mall an attendant/an older very old school mannish looking
Black woman walked in/stood next to me/stared
at me in the mirror
and in a quiet voice said
light skinned as you are
and with that good hair/looking like you do
you can have any woman you wants.

can get them to give you money and things too   if you know how.
she then gave the counter a quick wipe
turned and walked away.
friendly advice i suppose/from one stud to another.
fortunately for me
i grew up surrounded by femme power/and in that environment
grew into my butchness/from the inside out.
although i have had to look at ways that i've internalized sexism
    growing up
my butchness/my personal power has never been based on my
ability to manipulate or physically overpower and control women.

i have always been surrounded by femmes/was raised by one
my mother
single/migrated from the south to los angeles
she and all her friends were fierce femmes   come to the big city
to make a new life.
i adored these women/and they loved me—encouraged me to grow
fully into myself
relieved i believe
that i was more interested in sneakers shorts and playing ball/than
finding the path to womanhood as they understood it.
although men were not intricately woven into my daily life/they
    were around.
i watched them use their physical power/the privilege of their male-
    ness
in an effort to control my mother and her friends.
i saw that the femmes out-thought these men/played them for
whatever points they wanted/while envisioning building and main-
taining their own lives
and the lives of their children
all the while working/giving into/and sometimes being dominated

by male ego and pride. i saw myself more like those butch men than the femmes that raised me/though i did not like the way the men underestimated talked down to and mistreated the femmes.
i understand now that the very conservative south they had all fled from/was present somehow within the confines of the female-male games they played/that these men had very little power outside of the homes they lived in and visited and that jim crow had preceded my family moving west/imposing continued separate but not equal housing education and employment opportunities.
living in this kind of reality
trying to survive
things got buried
unnamed
unspoken
forgotten
masked/forced
tossed out
boiled over/burned.
and often
simply evaporated.

naming myself/butch gave me a lens to look through/a way to speak on explore and understand my experiences and feelings.
i don't believe that i have to model my behavior after men. i be-lieve that if men had the freedom to be fearlessly who they are/if this world didn't punish the feminine more men/and more butches would live inside their sensitivity speaking from the heart/deeply feeling/willing and able to communicate quickly clearly powerfully truthful   there would be more Peace.
but that is not the world we live in.

once
an older femme woman/a seer came up to me
said
gurl
you was a man last life.
yes
but you was soooo bad to the wy'mns
that they sent you back a wo'mn this time yourself.
and you begged and pleaded/cause you didn't want to be no
wo'mn
but they said you had to be taught
so here you are
and that's why you got so much man energy
uhmmhum
yes.
so now i'm telling you
you better be nice to the wy'mns.
are you nice to the wy'mns! do you have a wo'mn!
well
you better be nice.
else you gonna come back a wo'mn again/next time.

yes ma'am.
i am trying.
i am trying to be nice to the womens.
and i am trying to be nice to me/the woman the man the butch.

as a butch/i have often felt like i'm an easily identifiable lesbian-
target for closeted and curious women looking to play. this used
to upset me/until i admitted that i was choosing to be with these
kinds of women—unavailable women/women who could not or
would not

love me completely and openly.
as a result
my heart was never not broken/so
i was always loving from a place of resentment.
deep down
i didn't think that i would ever find someone that would be with me
stay/and truly love me.
furthermore i realized that i carried shame everywhere i went
because there was a way that i felt humiliated every day almost
every place i went.
from public bathrooms to public stores/where people assuming me
a young Black man targeted their hate and mistrust of young Black
men toward me/following me with distrust and fear. marking me a
thief a thug/not human. and some
people assuming me a gay man or a lesbian targeted their
heterosexism toward me. and some people seeing me working-class
decided me not worthy of the time of day.
and i remembered that as i grew older
from a tomboy to a wo'mn/called sir
fear and embarrassment changed my mother's ability to love me
   unconditionally.
i realized that i have carried the weight of my mother's disapproval/
   silently
unknowingly for as long as i can remember
i have responded to her disappointment and shame.
it has been the whisper of doubt/the murmur of guilt
the worrying reason/part of why
i've never looked in the mirrors
i haven't lived in my own body completely
i have embodied butch-phobia.
i realized that i wanted my mother's approval.
i had been waiting

to hear
you look good today
congratulations/you did great today   daughter i'm so proud of you.
words that i will probably never hear
from my mother.

today i say
SO WHAT!
i love my mother and i know she loves me.
i can't continue to blame her or anyone else for the resentment that
i embody and put out
in the world/in relationships. once i stopped blaming the women in
my life for all my
problems/once i decided to commit to learning to love myself
slowly i began to Heal/to honor my own
heart
scars and all
and to live/from the inside out
in my
butchness.

today
butch fits me like a box/a label too small to express all of who i am.
today i say i am two-gendered.
but that's a whole nutha story/yeah....

Greys

D. Travers Scott

Succumbing to the inherent truth of clichés ranks as one of the suckiest aspects of bachelorhood. Clichés converged on me after the fadeout of the relationship in which I'd spent nestled for nearly my entire twenties. "Discover yourself." "Pick yourself up by your bootstraps." "You can't love anyone new until you learn to love yourself." These trite homilies—acutely grating to a twenty-nine-year-old confirmed cynic—comprised not only the constant advice of earnest friends, but—far worse—the truths I discovered on insomniac nights of soul-searching, hoarse-throated crying jags with my ex, or risky and revealing conversations with my parents.

With this ongoing examination, I've discovered human relations don't seem to complexify; they simplify: I need my space. You have to trust people. Life is hard.

The "lightbulb moment," when I realized that many truths are themselves as clichéd as the phrase "lightbulb moment," came as a sinking feeling rather than glorious epiphany. While this realization may have in fact evidenced wisdom—I'm in my thirties now, and not yet certain enough to stake claim to that particular attribute—it nevertheless sucked ass.

If there was a bright side to ending ten years of love and commitment in the middle of the holiday season, this realization of the truth in clichés should have been it. For over a year I'd been working on a new book about embracing clichés, overcoming the jaded cynicism spoon-fed to my generation. It was to be a collection of interviews—opportunities to talk, share, and become vulnerable with people beyond my secure orbit. It would put my newfound realizations to the test. I would endeavor to rediscover and reinvigorate places in my world for hope, idealism, respect, and heroes. You know: hackneyed clichés.

Online I discovered an Alaskan family who lived one hundred miles from the nearest airport, and they considered this cushy. For twenty-plus years they'd lived in the bush, in isolated hand-built cabins. While not working odd jobs like fire fighting and rescue work, the father taught his kids to hunt caribou and other game. The mother ran a tight ship of a house and was a writer herself. They were devout Christians living in a separatist, self-sustaining Christian community.

Via email, I first contacted the mother. We corresponded for several months. She was understandably wary of this stranger wanting conversation with her family.

She was also tempted. I was a published novelist, and she was a struggling author shopping around several books, which were good, and I was sincerely interested in helping her. I introduced her to my agent and offered frank advice from my experiences in publishing.

I explained my project to her, how it was about learning to take risks, to be vulnerable with people, and to dare to seek the rewards that might come from that. I was searching for people to look up to, be inspired by, and to have as role models. I thought her family might be such people. I meant it. My sentiments were sincere, if awkward. After all, I'd grown up during the Watergate-Iran/Contra-Lewinsky timeline.

She started feeling me out, asking about my family and religion. I told her the truth: my childhood instruction in faith had been a contradictory combination of Southern Baptist, agnostic, and New Age neo-pagan, leaving me in something of a muddle, but respectful of all faiths.

To my shock, she invited me to join her family for a weekend. They had a cabin they'd built outside their house; I could stay there. They would show me their land, their old homestead, their trapping cabins, the Christian community, the sled dogs, and we could talk. I agreed quickly.

With the holidays coming, we had to plan fast. I reserved a flight only two weeks away. During that time, she looked up the titles of my novels and a forthcoming book I'd edited. When she asked about them, admittedly I glossed over the goriest details—a bi-teen ménage à trois and the performance-art peep shows—yet I was forthright in their themes and intents and other projects of mine, racier aspects included.

Mere days before departure, she wrote back saying that she was concerned. While I could still come visit, she would withhold her permission for me to write about her family until after my visit. I emailed her the introduction to the book in progress, so she could clearly see the context within which I hoped her family would appear. I'd already long ago sent her the five-page proposal and outline.

I hesitated before hitting the send button. A brief section of the book's introduction mentioned I was gay. She and I had previously danced around this subject when she'd asked if I was married. I said no (true, and truer every day). I didn't offer up that I couldn't be married if I wanted to. She didn't probe further with questions she could easily have asked, such as, "Do you have a girlfriend? How does romantic love fit into the ideals of your book? What about marriage?"

Days before Christmas, I landed at the small Alaskan airport right after the 3:30-p.m. sunset. Greys colored this world: skies, snow, clouds, slush. The thin air kept the trees' height below twenty feet. The massive, snow-filled sky dwarfed the runt evergreens. On the hour-and-a-half drive to their cabin from the airport, the husband

and I got acquainted, talking about everything from Alaskan history to the Clinton impeachment trial. I was surprised by the degree to which we concurred, and enjoyed his company.

The mother was making dinner when we arrived. As I entered their hand-built log house decorated with mounted animal heads and pelts, Christmas lights, and aquariums, she ran over and embraced me.

"I've been reading the introduction you sent me," she said, beatific, "and it's just wonderful. I can't tell you how much I agree with what you're doing." She turned to her husband and said, somewhat sternly, "This man is a very great writer."

She referred to me during dinner as her friend.

I felt flushed with excitement. *It's working!* My project was working. I was forging a bond, a connection with people far outside my urban, gay, middle-class, artsy liberal enclave. Focusing on essentials could surmount differences. I ate their homemade food and looked through their hunting scrapbooks, proud of myself and excited about the new people in my life. As if on that fifth or sixth date when you dare to acknowledge more-than-casual feelings for someone, I dared to feel that I'd found new friends, that here were people I could respect, look up to, and trust. These were risky behaviors that didn't come easily to me, but I knew I had to become better versed in them for any future relationship to last.

I bedded down in their smaller adjacent cabin, and a wood stove kept me warm. Wolf-husky half-breeds howled outside in the thirty-below cold. I worried about how she had said that she had *started*, but hadn't *finished* reading my introduction. The gay section was near the end. What if she finished reading it tonight?

I told myself I was being urban and heterophobic, expressing the same disdain for conservatives and religious fundamentalists who I'd always been quick to attack in fellow art school or literati peers. When conservative Christians are bashed, I'm quick to point out that

I come from a family of conservative Christians, and they've shown me a lot more support and love than many of my queer brethren.

Besides, I thought, if they both read the intro, and it's okay, think what an even better story this will make.

Early in the morning darkness, the husband came and woke me up. We talked for quite a bit. He was more confused than hostile; homosexuality was simply outside his experience. He asked his wife to join us and we three talked some more. She was adamant: I couldn't write about them. She didn't want my help getting her own work published. (My agent had already expressed an interest in her.) I had to leave immediately after breakfast.

When I acquiesced to her wishes, she presented me with another option.

"I think you were brought here for a reason," she told me. "We have tools. We have ways of dealing with your problem. Evil spirits are real, and we have ways of attacking them. You can stay—if you'll repent and submit to our help."

I told her I would skip breakfast. They could take me to the airport now.

That didn't fit into their plans, so we sat down to homemade berry pancakes. Mine came with an extra helping of humiliation. (Have I mentioned I was coming out of a ten-year relationship? That my ex was already dating one of our friends? That in the previous month an angry writer had attacked me as a racist in an email distributed to all of my family, friends, and business contacts? That I was turning thirty?) In front of their kids, the husband and wife were down-home cheery. We ate and chatted; I accompanied the husband and kids into town, waited while they ran errands, and finally was dropped off at the tiny airport.

The smiling face/stab-in-the-back was a cliché of conservative Christians cited by my urbane gay friends. "They hate fags as a group, but they can love individuals. That's how you have to channel your activism: one person at a time."

The last I heard from this family came a year later. A media blitz had alerted the world to Melissa, a computer virus globally infecting thousands of systems. Within weeks, it arrived in my inbox. I was startled to see that telltale header, "Important Message From—" but more startled by the send address: the Alaskan family.

I opened the message and, sure enough, there was the infected Microsoft Word attachment and the pirated alphabetical list of address book entries. In their self-imposed media isolation, the Alaskan family obviously hadn't heard the warning.

I gloated a little. "Ha! Stupid Christians, that's what you get for putting your heads in the sand."

However, I was taken aback by the fact that I was still in their address book. After being ejected from their home, one of the first things I'd done upon returning was to delete them from mine.

Why Point Out What We Already Know?

Chong-suk Han

Small talk with gay men I meet is like a river with many tributaries that all flow into the same delta. No matter how it starts or where it winds, I'm inevitably asked about the big O. "How long have you been out?" Or its fraternal twin, "How out are you?"

In the Western narrative of what it means to be "gay," coming out, that pivotal moment when one goes from being unsure, afraid, or ashamed, to being proud of one's sense of self, is mythically defined as the moment of rebirth into a new life.

Just as the O question is predictable, so is the narrative that accompanies the answer. Always marked by various stages of denial, internal conflict, and eventual acceptance, the journey of sexual self-discovery for a gay man is envisioned to culminate in the cathartic moment when he confidently proclaims to the world that he is gay—"coming out of the closet." Coming out is thought to be not only a matter of publicly acknowledging one's sexual preference, but also a reflection of an individual's positive appraisal and commitment to *being* gay in a heterosexual society—whatever that might mean.

To come out, then, is to mark oneself as a specific type of person, one who takes on a specific type of identity, one who leads a specific type of life. Coming out is so important that asking someone how out they are is like asking them how gay they are. Asking them when they came out is like asking them when they were born. Some men I know celebrate it as a second birthday, much like former alcoholics who mark the end of one life and the beginning of the next. If you're not out entirely, then you're simply not gay enough.

The problem here isn't the nature of coming out or of living out and proud all the time. All the more power to those who do it. The problem is the belief among many gay men that not coming out is a mark of shame and denial. According to *The Gay Almanac*, being in the closet is considered "the *confining* state of being secretive about one's homosexuality." The problem is the way that some of us who live out loud judge those who do not. For too many gay men, there is a clear line between being out and "hiding." Sometimes, they believe so strongly in the power of being out that they deliberately out others. But is this dichotomy between being out and being closeted so easy to draw?

For me, and for many other men I've met in my life, being "gay" is a constant negotiation rather than a momentary declaration that changes one's life forever. Rather than being "out and proud all the time," gay Asian men vacillate between being "gay," being "Asian," and being "gay and Asian," depending on the situation. While one can easily read this vacillation as being out when convenient and hiding when not, such an argument would simply reinforce the very Western notion that not focusing on my gayness as being my central identity somehow diminishes my life overall.

From my perspective as a gay man of color, the problem of putting such importance on coming out, being out, and living out reinforces the Western notion that there is only one way to be gay—and that all other ways of being gay, obviously including mine, are simply not enough. It's as if, once we decide to be gay, we have to leave all our other identities behind. I see this often with gay white men. Once they come out of the closet, they sever all ties with their former self. Almost overnight, all of their friends are gay, all of their activities are gay, and all of their support systems are gay. But not all of us have the comfort of seamlessly entering the gay community. For some of us, the entry is rather bumpy.

Many gay activists like to believe that there aren't issues of racism within the gay community; they like to think that they are above oppressing others. These folks are not simply blind, they are deluded. Looking around any gayborhood, any gay magazine, or any other place where "gay" is visible, one thing becomes blatantly clear—"gay" is very, very white.

Certainly, gay men of color will tell you stories of explicit racism in the gay community range from being excluded from leadership roles in gay organizations to being denied entrance to gay bars. But for me, explicit racism is easy. You can point to it, name it, and then fight it.

Subtle forms of racism are a bit more difficult. Racism in its subtle form seeks to erase the experiences of non-white folks, whether gay or not. It's about not seeing myself in gay magazines and being told at gay meetings not to muddy the waters by trying to interject issues of race and racism and confusing them with gay issues. But the most subtle is being told exactly how I should be gay. In the Western narrative of what it means to be gay, it isn't enough simply to be happy with the person we are, but we must also actively accost others with our happiness.

"What do you mean you've never told your mother?" my gay white friends ask me. It's more than a question, it's an accusation: *"How could you not tell your mother?"*

The better question for me is, "Why in the world would I?"

A friend who also never "told" his mother summed it up best when he said, "For me, telling my mother that I'm gay would be like telling her that the sky is blue and expecting her to be surprised. I know I'm gay, she knows I'm gay. We don't routinely spend time pointing out the obvious."

I've never sat down with my mother and had the "Guess what, Mom" discussion. But to be fair, I don't think my sister ever sat her down to explicitly tell her that she's straight. Yet somehow, my mother figured out that her daughter is straight and that her son is gay. She asks about my "friend" and tells me never to move to Wyoming; yes, Matthew Shepard's horrible death even made it to the Korean cable news channel. I just don't think discussing my sex life is high on her list of things to do; I certainly have no desire to discuss hers. If I ever wake up one morning straight, then I'll call my mother. That would be news.

For me, strongly identifying with my Asian identity has always provided me with a healthy sense of self-worth, long before it dawned on me that I like men. The lessons I learned as a racial minority in an often-racist society gave me the armor to combat the racism I see in the gay community. Am I expected to give up that part of my life? Should I relinquish that part of my identity?

Leaders in the gay community argue repeatedly about needing to be inclusive. Perhaps what we really need is a new way of measuring "gayness" other than our willingness to live "out and proud" all the time. The belief that for gay men to be truly happy, they must confront others with their gay identity, privileges a Western view of what it means to be gay. Focusing on coming out as the universal requirement to *being* gay puts the experiences of gay white men at the center while pushing the experiences of other gay men to the margins. Of course, there are countless numbers of gay Asian men who have actively come out to their friends, their families, the guy at the market, etc. Many of my gay Asian friends, even those who have not yet had the *Guess what, Mom* talk, feel a tremendous amount of pressure to engage in that conversation. But I wonder if they ever ask themselves why. Is it for them, their families, or does it fit the Western model of what it means to be gay?

Certainly, we shouldn't have to hide who we are from anyone. But is there only one way of *being* who we are? I've never told a single person in my family that I'm gay, yet somehow, everyone knows. More importantly, nobody cares. If I told them, they would have to confront what that means in a very public way, and confrontation is so Western. I just don't see any need or benefit of pointing out to my mother that the sky is blue.

Breath

Achy Obejas

It is 1978 in central Indiana. There is snow on the ground. I'm lying across the front seat of a large American car, its doors wide open, with a woman who is resting her head on my bare stomach. The way I'm lying, I see the sky—a grey, colorless palette. When I push my head back, I see the ground, upside down. We're in a cemetery, rows of rough slabs interrupted by bouquets spilling pale colors. Though it's cold enough to guarantee snow, we had to open the doors to get some fresh air so I could breathe. The car smells of sex, of bittersweet sweat. My thighs are sticky from the woman's saliva and my own come.

It's my second-year anniversary. Not with the woman who has spent this afternoon making love with me, but with Diane, who's making dinner back at our cramped apartment. Diane is my first adult lover, the first woman I've ever really been in love with, the first woman who has returned all my passions, the first person I've lived with outside my family. She's half-Welsh, half-Lebanese, with a volcanic temper and blue daggers for eyes.

We have an open relationship, out of terror, although when we talk about it we have a fabulous political explanation for our arrangement. We mention patriarchy and the oppression of women, discuss finding new ways of relating. We don't talk about being jealous or hurt, or wanting to last forever. We wouldn't dare say we are devastated by how much we might mean to each other, or that we dread being abandoned.

I am twenty-one years old, as thin and pliable as a reed. Diane takes my photograph and pins the pictures everywhere: the fridge, the bathroom mirror, the car's visor. I have never felt so desired, so sexually potent, so enamored of myself. As I languidly lie in the car, I realize I'll be late for my anniversary dinner. It doesn't occur to me to call. I'm absolutely sure—not that it's okay—but that I'll be forgiven.

It is summer 1990 and, on my thirty-fourth birthday, my lover of five mostly monogamous years informs me that she's having an affair. She tells me in the car, on the way back from the airport, where I've just picked her up from visiting this other woman.

Later, I'm lying on the couch with my face in the cushions, trying to drown out the sounds around me, trying to find the rhythm of my own breathing. My lover has locked herself in the bathroom, where she is conducting what feels like a marathon telephone conversation with her new lover. I can't hear what they're saying, but her laughter filters through the walls and unnerves me.

I can't sleep now. I forget to eat. I tell myself that I must be patient, that I have the moral ground of a postage stamp in which to maneuver and protest, that what I need to do is exhibit exemplary behavior and then all of this new lover stuff will come to a halt.

I learn to count to ten in Arabic, as an exercise: *waid, itnayn, zalaza....* And I begin to think about Diane. A lot.

It's winter 1991 and I've begun to write letters to Diane, all of them in my head:

Dear Diane,

You told me that, eventually, after I got hurt enough, I'd learn the value of gesture. It's taken me thirteen years but I'm beginning to get it....

You never said I should have called—your own forgiving gesture—but I should have. My lover shouldn't have told me about the affair in the car, on my birthday, without telling me first that she loved me.

Where are you? Last I heard, you were living in Boston. Do you still take photographs? Fuck your lovers until they beg for breath?

I'm going through some boxes in my closet and discover one filled with correspondence from Diane. One postcard, illustrated with primary colors, reads: "Lie in my arms bleeding, loved one." I laugh to myself, a little embarrassed. Did we really say things like that to each other?

Back then I thought we were the only two women who had ever felt that near delirium. Can I confess something? Every morning, I marveled that you were still there, all tangled up with me. I was such a brat. Why in heaven's name did you stay? These days, I marvel that my ex-lover didn't stay. I loved her so much and, generally speaking, I was so well-behaved.

When a friend comes over, she sees Diane's letters spread out on the kitchen table and asks about them. I show her a few of the postcards, read her a poem. I figure whatever the statute of limitations on privacy is, it's up by now. There's a photograph of me from back then, on Diane's bed, my wrists tied up in lace, my lips so red it looks like I'm cut. And there's a photograph of Diane, years after we broke up, pregnant and naked, blue veins like rivers on her swollen breasts, her eyes a gale of anger and love. She's holding a pomegranate split in two, its seeds oozing. I immediately conclude that we were too weird, that no one in the world is going to get it without laughing at us, so I start to put everything away.

"My god," says my friend, "you two were so lucky."

Dear Diane,

For the record, it hurt like hell that you refused to see me, refused to talk to me after we broke up. I thought you were being spiteful, petty. I didn't get why things had to be so final. Years later, when I had to track you down because your mother was dying and your family didn't know where you were, you wouldn't come to the phone. "What do you want?" you hissed, finally. Your voice cut right through me. That's the first time I felt the full force of your pain.

It's spring in an undetermined year and I'm at bar on the west side of Chicago with a bisexual actress who's flirting with me. She's picking out tunes on the jukebox, songs like "Can't Help Falling in Love," "Carmen," and "Walking After Midnight." Finally, she asks me what I'd like to play. I scan the songs and mumble something that comes out like "Wooly Bully." She has rendered me stupid. She pulls me to her for a kiss—a performance of sorts for her friends, who watch avidly—and jams my hand under her skirt, where it's murky and moist. I go along, but it only makes me remember how long it's been since I've really wanted to kiss somebody.

Dear Diane,

You always thought I was so cool, but I think that was just because you loved me so much. The fact is, I lack the hardness, the opaque quality necessary to pretend I want anything other than love.

I remember once you showed me a collection of women's still-lifes. They were smaller than men's paintings, and more crowded. You pointed out the bruises on the banana, the fly on the tomato. You said men were romantics, women were realists. You said women knew nothing was ever perfect; nothing was ever won without a fight. You said I'd eventually understand the rewards.

Then you told me I was a boy trapped in a dykelet's body. I didn't talk to you for a week after that. You called every day, trying to apologize, but I wouldn't answer. Back then, I thought every fight was final, every difficulty an impossibility. I wasn't trying to be cool, you know; I wasn't trying to make you work that hard. I was just scared, that's all.

You told me that opportunity isn't endless, that love isn't random, and that we'd be picking pieces of each other off ourselves for the rest of our lives. I thought you were so damn dramatic. I had no notion you were so right.

It's winter 1996 and I get a letter from a gay man who used to live not far from that cramped apartment Diane and I nested in so many years ago. He has been writing her in India since she moved but all his letters have been returned. When I investigate, the American consul tells me Diane has been murdered. The killing, unsolved, is too gruesome to describe.

Dear Diane,

Do you remember that time you asked me to choke you, to wrap my fingers around your neck and push with all my might, how I went to my task so arduously, and you were kicking beneath me, stabbing me with your nails (I still have the half-moon scars on my wrists), until you threw me on the floor—I smashed against the bookshelves, toppled a vase—and you went into spasms, choking and coughing. You were red, slippery with spit and mucous, furious with me: "Don't you know," you screamed, your voice cracking, "don't you know you're supposed to say 'There's enough pain in the world already—what the hell would I do without you'?"

It's too late, but I know, I know now.

The Modernist Chair: A Short History

Robin Metcalfe

Edmonton 1974

> "Eero Aarnio's Ball Chair isolates its user within a
> large, low, shiny sphere, blocking out both sight and
> sound from all but the frontal direction.... Its fully
> upholstered interior creates a hushed, self-contained
> environment...."
> —Kathryn B. Heisinger and George M. Marcus,
> *Landmarks of Twentieth-Century Design: An Illus-*
> *trated Handbook*

I am a sucker for Modernism. If it has clean, sinuous lines and owes
its existence to Charles or Ray Eames, Russell Wright, or anyone
named Eero, I have to have one. I still savor the moment when I told
my friend Susan S., who shares this passion, that I had acquired an
Ericofon (L.M. Ericsson, Sweden, 1956), that impossibly elegant upright sculptural telephone with a dial hidden under its base. "Please
tell me it's not green," Susan S. pleaded. "I couldn't stand it if you
found a green one." Of course it's green. If your friends won't recognize your good fortune with bitter envy, who will?

I will go further and say I am a cocksucker for Modernism. I came
out around Easter in 1974, more or less exactly in one of Eero Aar-
nio's swivelling Ball Chairs (Finland, 1965) in the Edmonton Public
Library. If you imagine acrobatic contortions inside a silver sphere,
I must disappoint you. However, I am forever in the debt of some

enlightened librarian who had stocked the Homosexuality section with the latest, post-Stonewall literature. When I finally took the bull of my desire by its literary horns and braved the terrors of the card catalogue's *H* subject section, there were "Eminent Authorities" to assure me, as I sat cradled with a recent sociology text in my upholstered steel pod, that I had licence to do what I wanted with my eager twenty-year-old butt.

Shortly after this, I moved into the basement of a suburban-style home on Saskatchewan Drive, not far from the University. One bath, three bedrooms. One bedroom was empty and the other was home to a proto-feminist named Claire who quickly became the first new friend of the officially gay me. She even let me draw her, semi-nude, in one of the more private glades of Queen Elizabeth Park.

On the eighth of June, as recorded in my diary, I heard someone moving into the third room. I introduced myself to my neighbor; I will call him Brent. A little later, coming back from a walk, I met Claire at the top of the stairs, who told me, with salacious satisfaction, that she thought Brent was gay.

Brent came to my room for the first of many talks. I found out that he, like I, was half-French, as his last name made clear. He came from a northern forestry town, home to a large Métis population. His hair was dark, with fine curls, but I remember skin as pale as alabaster, high cheekbones under large, dark, soulful eyes. He was intelligent and we could talk about the Big Subjects that fascinated the young in 1974. I thought I'd get along with him very well.

With youthful perversity, I resisted Claire's assumption that Brent and I would soon be making the two-backed beast. Several days followed of conversations, walks through Queen Elizabeth Park to the banks of the North Saskatchewan River, listening to each other's music, eating each other's food. On the tenth of June we walked across the High Level Bridge, talking about revolutions and death, favorite subjects for those who have little experience of either.

Two days later it was his birthday and I tried to cheer him up when he said he felt "dumpy." And on the fourteenth, not quite a week after Claire's prediction, I went into his room still damp from a bath and we made love for the first time. "I felt completely fine," I told my diary, in wonder. "He is very beautiful."

Thus began my first true affair of the heart, where that organ acts in league with the lips, the fingers, and the cock. It began in the White Nights of a northern summer, when the sky never truly darkens and the sunset lingers below the horizon like a guest who does not want to leave. I was luckier than most to have Brent Ladouceur as my first taste of love. He was sweet and smart, and as green and eager as I was.

Summer is glorious in Edmonton, but the winter is dark and hard and I was not planning to stay for another one. The day we walked across the bridge, I had received a letter from the art college back home and by the end of August I was on my way back to Halifax. The knowledge that I was leaving may have given us the freedom to love for the time we did. After my return east, our contact faded. I remember hearing of a boyfriend in Calgary who took him mountain climbing, and then I lost touch.

Halifax 2004

> "As visitors entered the exhibition, they were immediately confronted with a moulded armchair, made ... in Vancouver. This piece of furniture embodied a Scandinavian aesthetic...."
> —Alan C. Elder, *Designing a Modern Identity: The New Spirit of British Columbia, 1945–60*

It was a cold February the next time I returned to Halifax after living away. I'd worked three years for an art museum in London, Ontario—a city I never loved, although one where I made many friends. I arrived back in Halifax to take a position as director and curator of a university art gallery the same week the city received the greatest snowfall on record, anywhere, in any urban center: a meter of snow in a single day.

A couple of weeks after that white avalanche, I came across Brent's name in a catalogue of contemporary furniture design from British Columbia, where Modernism flourished after World War II. Brent appeared as a cofounder of a chic little design company with a funky name. I Googled it, and sent the company an email asking if this was the same Brent Ladouceur I had known in Edmonton in 1974. His business partner graciously replied: "Yes. Our Brent is your Brent." He was sorry to have to add that Brent had died of AIDS six years earlier. "I should add that he was more than my business partner— we were together for fourteen years. (So I have heard tales....) He would have welcomed your attempt to contact him."

London 2006

> "The first fiberglass chair to be mass-produced, Eero
> Saarinen's armchair was hailed as revolutionary when
> it appeared on the American market in 1948."
> —Heisinger and Marcus

I was back in London, Ontario, in July 2006, visiting an ex-boyfriend and catching up with other friends. Prominent among them was Susan E.—not to be confused with Susan S., although both Susans lived in the Old South in homes that were museums of modern design. A curator like myself, Susan E. had arrived in London from out west just before I had decamped for the east, and we both regretted the lost chance to get better acquainted. A supper at her home on a fine July night was to make up for that missed opportunity.

The house, as my journal records, was "elegantly spare without being frigid, full of high-design objects from the 1950s and 1960s, a collection that overlaps with my own and Susan S.'s." We drank lots of wine and had fat tender chunks of organic barbecued beef as we gossiped about museum colleagues and she described a project she was doing in Japan with an artist who interested us both.

As the evening was winding up, I admired a chair in her front room, which I took for an Eero Saarinen Womb Chair of 1948, one that someone had lovingly rescued and reupholstered in a grey fabric with randomly scattered rectangles. The other Susan had reportedly disapproved of the upholstery as inauthentic, but Susan E. said she would never change it. As I relaxed in its generous curves, she told me she'd acquired it from two of her best friends in Vancouver, a gay couple with a furniture business. She could never change it, because "Brent Ladouceur upholstered that chair."

Ghosts give no warning they are about to visit. For a moment, I was in two places at once. I was sitting in the home of charming friends at the end of a lovely evening full of good food, wine, and conversation. And I was pulled three decades back in an instant, embraced by the handiwork of a lost love, feeling a deep vein of sorrow open beneath the agreeable surface of the evening. There is no sharing that sudden loss of altitude, that elevator drop into private grief. Susan and I had lost the same person, but from opposite ends of a too-brief life. She grieved a man in the full flush of an achieved self, a creative professional in a loving partnership. Brent and I had met, loved and parted, on the threshold of lives we had barely begun to imagine.

I have no photograph of Brent. Somewhere, however, I have a

drawing I did of him. It's a nude, although decorously wrapped in a blanket from which his arms, shoulders, and tousled hair emerge, his face down-turned as if in reflection. At once lanky and fragile, he crouches like a bird who hesitates before taking flight.

Miss Scarlet, with Cat Poo, in the Castro

Kirk Read

My friend Karin is good with confrontation. She'll get in line for the express check-out, tap on someone's shoulder, and say, "That's way more than fifteen items." I'm from the South. We have to get drunk before that kind of toe-to-toe. Normally, that is. The other night, I snapped.

Okay, so this guy from an America Online chatroom invites me over to his house. We had an 8K conversation, which consisted of about twenty lines of an AOL chat document. I save all of them. I'm obsessive about filing them in an orderly fashion, with dates and screen names. Not that I have Glenn Close as "Alex the bunny boiler" aspirations. Just that I'm passionate. Not that I need medication, like most of my family. Not that I have been called out by exes for acting inappropriately toward them. Forget that.

I go there at eleven p.m. and ring his doorbell. I was meeting him for sex, natch. I admit it. I'm a loose woman, an adventurous lad. He told me to wear a coat and tie. We were going to do some sort of English schoolboy spanking scene. I'm kinky.

Boyfriend does *not* answer the door. The lights are out, the blinds are closed. Well, I've dealt with far too many of these AOL assholes. He's one of those rich queens with his own entrance in the Castro, you see.

So I get in the pickup truck and return home to make absolutely sure that I had the right address. I did. But while driving home, every stoplight on Market Street made me angrier. And when I get really pissed off, I hear Jesse Jackson's voice in my head. When I get home, I clean out my cat's litter box, and with each scoop, I hear Jesse say,

"*I am somebody.*" I bag the shit up and I get back into that truck and return to his house.

I was out there defending every gay man in this world from bad sexually confused behavior. I'm a hero, really. You should thank me.

The TV is spilling four shades of blue through the front door window. That queen thought I'd left. But no. I lean on the buzzer for fifteen minutes and nothing happens. I am a thoughtful criminal; I have latex gloves and packing tape. I watch *Cops*; I'm not naïve. I tape a pebble over his buzzer so that it will keep ringing all night.

Finally, he comes out of the house and says, "I'm sleeping" in this pissy sort of French accent, which matches his online grammatical performance *exactly*.

And loud enough for neighbors to hear, I say, "You asked me over the SanFranciscoM4M room to come for an English schoolboy discipline scene." And he says, "I don't have AOL" in this whiny, faux-startled tenor, all innocent. If he had a fan made of feathers, he would have shaken it.

Then he says, "You'd better get out of here before I call the cops," and closes the door. And I spread that feline manure all over his front step, right under the outside gate. I AM ... SOMEBODY.

One of the common mistakes you hear about criminals is that they often revisit the scene of the crime—for vanity or other reasons, including a desire to visually manifest the consequences of a spree.

Later, I drive by but don't see any change in the still life I'd left. No stomping of feet to shake free the doo-doo. No out on the landing dialing 9-1-1 on his cell phone. No hands on hips in the middle of the sidewalk, waiting for my return. Just the gentle blue light from his TV, wafting through the stained glass window above his doorway, and cars parked crookedly in front of his house, as they were earlier. Will I return in the morning? No. I'm done. God forbid I should stalk this poor man.

But I'm tired of apologizing and forgiving the bad behavior of men around matters sexual. I include myself in that group, because Lord knows I've behaved badly. Too many times, men online flake out or disappear, with no regard for your time or ego. Their sexual repression trumps your feelings. And you're stood up, or jerked around, or lied to. And I say that's no longer acceptable.

Societal and familial homophobia are not reasonable excuses to treat someone like an insurance sales representative. It's not okay to make an invitation to another human being and then back out of it without appropriate prior communication. It's not okay to participate in the raising of someone's pheromones, only to retreat without warning. I say this as someone who is guilty guilty guilty. I'm amazed there isn't catshit on my front doorstep every day.

But this isn't about my bad behavior, it's about the bad behavior of others. Let's stick to that particular angle of this story. I don't want to hover too much in the area of "Kirk's incorrect conduct"; how self-reflective can one be when one is leaving kitty dung on the front porches of complete strangers?

I don't mean plural strangers, actually. It was a rhetorical usage of strangers. There's only one. Tonight. With a French accent. In a house with a basement garage. Unshared by other tenants. Not that I'm embittered by his opulence, when I live in a town where all the young people live with eighteen roommates. Never mind the fact that he can afford the luxury of "no" and feel protected by police when I attempt to let him know that his prank of human contact went unappreciated.

We as gay people need to address these matters of incivility with swift reminders that we will not tolerate mistreatment. By any means necessary, we must step up our arsenals of wit and creative retribution.

Say with me, children: I will not be stood up. I will not let the flakes fake me out. I will not shrug off my hurt feelings and pretend in the morning that it didn't happen. I will fight back. I will march! I will fight back with kitty turds and obscene phone calls and dead roses. I will not be deterred by potential police scrutiny. I will not be derailed by the possibility that observant neighbors could turn into character witnesses. I shall not be moved. Say with me, children: "*I shall not be moved.*"

So this guy, right? He gave me this nasty look before he closed the door. Sort of like he was disgusted by me.

I hope in the morning he falls on his ass. The next time he invites someone to get in his car and drive to his home late at night for sex, I hope he means it.

As Jesse would say, "Keep hope alive."

Threats

Arden Eli Hill

On testosterone, and holding hands with my friend Emma, I don't look like as much of a fag as I am. Emma and I are downtown walking in the night heat talking about literature when guys in a passing pickup shout, "Hey, man! Why don't you get your girlfriend to show us her tits?"

I've been the target of enough street comments to know that people like that never want an answer. Sometimes guys drive by and make the blowjob sign at my boyfriend and me by joining their index finger to their thumb and jabbing at their mouths. They don't really want a blowjob. They certainly don't want to give one.

Emma and I keep walking and the night is full of other walking men, mostly single, mostly drunk. They nod hello, wishing me a good night or asking in slurred voices, "How's it going?"

"Good," I reply. There is little tension between them and me.

Emma turns to face me and says, "It's different being a girl."

I tell her, "I remember."

The brotherhood of strangers is invested in distance. Hellos are just a way of sounding across the canyon. A hello comes back, but it merely emphasizes the space; it does not bridge it. When I walk alone, I am every man's friend, a decent-looking kid with a smile. I worry that when strange men on the street look at Emma, they want to cross space, to grope, bruise, or fuck. I remember the words "broken broom" and "bottle," the sharp irony of "screwdriver handle." I remember, also, that this has happened to the boys that I love. That this could happen to me if I am fag-bashed or tranny-bashed after an assailant realizes there is an extra hole to stick it in.

The imagery of American society encourages female-bodied people to fear strange men, and I do at times, even though I am read as male. When I used the women's bathroom, I read on flyers, "A woman's highest risk of assault comes from a man deemed nice enough to be let into the house." But an ex-girlfriend has been the only partner to hit me. Another ex, one who has a domestic abuse hotline card on her refrigerator, failed to give me back my carved greenstone after we broke up. It is an item I'm sure I mentioned second or third in a short list of things when she asked me, "What do you own that makes you feel safe?" There is a range of physical violence and emotional hurt. I am not on a simple side of it either. The last time I saw my ex-boyfriend, I was wild-eyed, incoherent, and not yet on anti-psychotics. After a few days of silence, he ended our nine-month relationship by email, instructing me not to make eye contact if I saw him on the street.

Emma and I hug goodbye in the morning and I begin the drive back to school in Roanoke. Soon, a black SUV looms in my rear view mirror. I see a thick pale arm with the middle finger pointed up extending from the driver's side window. The SUV passes me, and although I look into the window, I can't see the driver's face. He shakes his fist, and in a quick motion, swerves directly in front of me. I can now make out a series of Navy bumper stickers on the huge rear-end of his vehicle.

I drive a Honda Civic that my mom termed an "asking-for-it-car." There is a "Be Green" sticker that I got from sending in a self-addressed stamped envelope and a macaroni and cheese lid. To the conservative eye, this might indicate that I am an eco-terrorist or at least a vegetarian. I have an "LGBT the T is not silent" sticker, but I doubt many people in the state know what the LGB, much less the T, even stand for. There is a sticker that advises, "Be Happy, Play

Rugby," but every gridiron fan knows that rugby is just football gone all queer. I have a rainbow stripe for the benefit of illiterate drivers. I proudly display the flag of New Zealand and a sticker of the Confederate flag with a red X through it. Text clarifies the insult, "You Lost, Get Over It." I have Massachusetts plates.

Now that the driver has passed me, I believe that the worst is over. He's shown his disapproval, he's cut me off, his ride is bigger than mine, and he's got a Hemi engine. The SUV switches lanes and then drops back behind me again. I check my gas and am glad to see the car has more than half a tank. The SUV picks up speed again, but instead of ramming me as its velocity and aim would suggest, it veers sharply, and now it's next to my car. The driver appears to have the ability to simultaneously drive, shoot the bird, and hurl French fries at my windshield. I turn my wipers on and they swish the fries away like two skinny arms in a desperate, "Oh shit, please don't hurt me" gesture. This continues until the driver is out of food.

I'm looking for a highway patrol station where I can pull over, but I don't know if he'd be on me before I could get inside, or even how sympathetic North Carolina's cops would be to the distress of anyone who is not a damsel. I decide my best option is to keep driving and wait for him to get tired of harassing me.

Thirty minutes later, every milligram of the anti-anxiety drug I took this morning has sweated out of my skin. I start creating excuses in my head: "Hey, man, it's my sister's car," or, "I really love pussy." That one would be easy enough to prove. The devil in my head whispers, "The truth doesn't set anybody free. Anything short of straight- and gender-conforming is queer enough to bash." Being trans means I don't even know who society believes I should love. I am certainly not encouraged to love myself. My enemy is three cars behind mine and my exit is approaching. I veer off of the highway. He doesn't follow.

"There is danger everywhere," my communities warned me, and I notice irony in my life. The last time I had a knife against my throat, I was the man holding it there. The first time I tried killing myself I was nine. My parents had taken me to a counselor because I did not "interact normally" with other children, but it was their constant fighting and the then undiagnosed mental illnesses that sat with me on the bathroom counter as I filled up the tub. The suicide attempt didn't work. I didn't know to put stones in the pockets of my nightgown.

I detail that episode from my childhood in a letter to a friend. He responds with the infuriating cliché, "Suicide is a permanent solution to a temporary problem." I have multiple diagnoses and take an anti-psychotic twice a day. I write back, "For me, suicide would be a permanent solution to a permanent problem." I concentrate on breathing.

While some guys report improved mental health after starting testosterone, I've been unaffected. I still cycle between highs and lows, though my suicidal times never coincide with an outside threat to my life. I can't imagine catching a glimpse of violence in the rearview mirror and pulling over, opening up the door, and not resisting as push comes to shove down on asphalt with my head home-running against a baseball bat.

In one depressed episode, I decided that if things weren't better in six months I was going to kill myself. Even then I knew I was bluffing, as I didn't write the date in my day planner. There are survival strategies I use—lying to myself, letting out a little blood, running miles, and taking the cranky elevator in the building where I work so that when it shakes, the desire for annihilation shifts into my body's need to bolt out of that unsteady thing. I conjure up the unreliable list of people who love me, but it barely helps. I call forth the more solid list of folks who hate me, and even when my own name is there at the top of the list, I harness that hate to fight wanting to die. I remember danger to call forth the desire for safety. My angels are usually little more than tufts of white feathers. I remember the threats that I am up against and I pit demon against demon when I am the most in need of salvation.

Dual Identities

Jane Van Ingen

A recent article in the *New York Times* talked about a portable so-
cial-cue reader, created by computer scientists at MIT's Media Lab,
which would help people with autism pick up on subtle visual cues.
Since people with autism have trouble with social interactions, the
device would help them decipher when someone is bored, annoyed,
sad, uncomfortable, etc. I discussed this device with a friend who
works with autistic children. She said that her kids who were high-
functioning enough to use the device probably wouldn't want to use
it, or they could be taught to read social cues and wouldn't need it.

As a lesbian with a profound hearing loss, I think the MIT device, although not entirely practical in everyday life, is an innovative
concept. I was born with a moderate hearing loss and the inability
to smell. Growing up, I was mainstreamed and wore hearing aids.
After college, I started losing more of my hearing for reasons that
are still unclear. In 1999, I had surgery for a cochlear implant, which
is akin to a customized listening device.

Although I'm very visual, I don't always pick up on auditory cues.
As a result, I am frequently worried that someone is calling me from
behind or that I'll leave the cashier before I pick up my receipt, and
I'm sometimes vigilant about clearly signing off before I end a phone
conversation. This is compounded by the fact that I live in New York
City, easily the loudest, most frantic city in the country. At times,
it takes me a minute or two to process what someone said. Even
in quiet situations, I am sometimes a beat or two behind in group
conversations. And it's not that I'm mousy: I love to talk. It's just
sometimes tricky to keep up with the flow of conversation.

This is not directly related to being a lesbian, which is secondary in my life. Ironically, I'm out to my family and friends, and at work to a lesser extent. I've written articles for LGBT publications, have volunteered for LGBT and AIDS groups, and volunteer for a lesbian archival organization. I don't advertise my sexuality, although if someone asks me, I will tell them. But coming out as a deaf woman, especially one with a cochlear implant who is not a part of the sign-language community, is harder. (The deaf, sign-language community tends to reject the notion of needing cochlear implants, feeling that they don't need to be "fixed.")

It's not that people are cruel and insensitive. Gay or straight, I've found that people can either work around my hearing loss or they can't. But I get tired of explaining myself, though I've learned over the years that I must. For example, I don't necessarily need things to be louder, I need things to be clearer. I'm always dismayed at how many television shows and DVDs aren't closed captioned. Yes, I can understand the TV without it, if I sit up and listen carefully. With closed captioning on, I can sit back and relax.

Another issue is that socializing revolves around bars and restaurants. Don't get me wrong, I love to eat at restaurants, but I don't love the noise that goes with it. Even many cafés are either noisy or shrouded in low lighting. I need to see someone's face when they're talking in a noisy or semi-noisy environment. Recently, someone planning a group outing told me they always go to quiet bars. Yes, I know bars are convenient meeting spots, especially for queer folks who aren't welcome everywhere, and I've frequented them with people I was dating after I was already comfortable with them. But trust me, there is no such thing as a quiet bar, especially when you are meeting a group of people for the first time.

I've gotten better at advocating for myself. I'll ask someone to repeat something that they said rather than let a comment go that I almost understood. At work, if I leave a message for someone with important information, I'll also fax or email it. I think I'm being clear, but people have informed me that sometimes my messages aren't, so I like to be thorough. If I'm going to a group outing where people are seated at a long table instead of a circular one, I always sit at the center so I can understand everyone. Or if someone has their hand in front of their mouth, I ask them to remove it so I can see their lips when they talk. But I don't always tell people that I have a hearing loss, and rarer still do I call myself deaf. If someone knows I have a hearing loss and they see I'm straining to understand them while they're talking, I'm less likely to speak up. I'm trying to get better at this, primarily because I don't expect people to read my mind.

It would be convenient if MIT created a device that spelled out auditory cues for me, although it wouldn't substitute for personal communication and understanding. It's been my experience that people without disabilities don't say anything for fear of offending me or being politically incorrect. (I'm no Pollyanna. I'm well aware that many people just don't care, so I avoid them when I can.) For many years, I was defensive about explaining my hearing loss, so this fear is not irrational. During the peak of my self-righteousness, I felt that it wasn't my job to explain hearing loss—or any other disability—to the ignorant masses.

But then I met other people with disabilities. A friend with a mild hearing loss has few issues with people knowing that she's a lesbian; she has a butch appearance but is a femme at heart. She is also forthright about her hearing loss—if she wore hearing aids, I'm pretty sure she would keep her hair short—whereas I will spend five minutes in front of the mirror making sure my implant doesn't peek through my hair.

When I first met her, she had been sober for more than fifteen years, but was having difficulty with her sobriety and had joined AA. I didn't understand why someone who had been sober for so long would join AA, and she patiently explained why. Then she started running an AA meeting that only had about six attendees. A year later, more than twenty people come to this meeting, and they frequently turn to her for advice.

It's not necessarily easier for people with physical disabilities, any more than it is for people who are openly queer. I was having brunch one day with a friend who uses crutches. A few minutes after the waiter brought me my chicken sandwich, he came over and asked us if we needed anything else. My friend said, "I would like my breakfast," and laughed pleasantly. The waiter was beside himself with apologies for not delivering her order and later said her pancakes were on the house. If the waiter had made the same mistake with me—and wait staff misunderstand me all the time—it's unlikely I would have received the same reaction.

One size does not fit all, for either the queer or disability community. People with disabilities need to advocate for themselves, no matter how tiresome it becomes. But people without disabilities are not completely off the hook. The next time you're interacting with an individual with a disability, find out what's going on in his or her head. Talk *with* them, not *at* them. Wouldn't you want someone to do the same for you?

Birds in the Hand

George K. Ilsley

Birds in the hand: age 26

The parakeet is a small social parrot native to Australia. In Australia, they travel in huge raucous flocks and can be agricultural pests. But the birds are not exported. All parakeets sold in Canada are raised in Canada, so the green and yellow, black-striped parakeet I saw flying in a Paris park was almost certainly from France, or somewhere near France. Hand-raised perhaps by Dutch or Flemish breeders and shipped to big city bird markets.

This parakeet in the park in Paris allowed me to capture him. To take him into my hand. He was young, and scared. I took him home. Carried the bird home in my hand. On the Métro, with a small social parrot, a native of Australia, rescued from the streets of Paris.

Later, I gave the bird to a Parisian lifeguard I'd somehow befriended. I had a pool pass and a Métro pass and explored Paris that way. Transit and city pools. And walking from one to the other.

An easy walk from Montmartre, through neighbourhoods characterized by desert people, there was a nicer, newer pool, not busy. This pool became my regular pool and other city pools became adventure destinations, excursions into the unknown and unpredictable. At the regular pool I knew the schedule and lap-swimming times and could go there and have a good swim.

At my regular pool, one of the lifeguards befriended me, because I was there all the time, pumping out hearty Canadian laps. And he was sitting there watching me.

This part is actually quite shocking: a girl almost drowned while the lifeguard was chatting me up. He was so friendly and inquisitive,

I wondered, *How did Parisians get their reputation as snobs?* His English and my French were equally bad, or equally good, we reached for consensus, and a young girl slipped unnoticed to the depth of the pool.

She was raised and resuscitated and I went back to my lengths.

A couple of weeks later the lifeguard invited me home for dinner. He lived in a dilapidated suburb I found extremely charming to visit. A large cracked mirror remains atmospheric. In the lifeguard's bed, I dreamt he left his body and swooped around the room, around and around in a whirl, with the two of us asleep on the bed in the middle like an eddy.

The remnant handles of chipped bowl-sized mugs are charming. Doors crooked in their frames are charming. A Parisian lifeguard is someone who insists my English accent is cute. (Everything was cute in Paris that summer, the word sadly overused, in English and in French. Still, I did not mind hearing that my "petit accent Canadien" was "cute.")

Eventually, I gave him the parakeet I found in the park. By then it had its own little cage and toys and was all set up.

Later it flew out his window and never looked back.

The greener grass: age 21

The first time my mother begged me not to leave her, I was stoned on hash oil and headed for Mexico.

It was the first time for hash oil, too. Allan had dipped a bent paper clip into the dark honey vial and smeared gobs of oil along a Zig Zag rolling paper. Blessed it with sprinkles of Drum, and rolled a droopy striped cigarette. No one called it a spliff. This was my hometown.

A year or two older than me, Allan was this boy who used to be one of the bad kids. A bad early bloomer. As a child, I was terrorized. Now at the pub, home from school for a visit, I could not understand why Allan was so friendly, glad to see me, keen to smoke me up. I began to see him as glaringly inconsequential, and in that same picture saw myself as someone who had—in a word—escaped. Escaped a similar fate just by leaving our rinky-dink hometown. I had got away.

The sensation of pity for a torturer swept over me. I used to be scared—now I felt sorry for someone so beaten and lost and so obviously stuck at the dead end he had rushed to achieve early in life. Maybe he sensed my mounting disinterest, maybe he'd had lots of experience with mounting disinterest, and that is why he brought out the dark honey vial.

Don't worry, he said, we can roll it up right here and then smoke it out back.

I was not used to hash oil. At first it was nothing, just a cigarette. And then it was something: a thick swelling rush of awareness, a buzz too complex, and I was really stoned. Too stoned to deal with Allan anymore, so I walked back to my parents' house.

Where everything was a thousand times worse.

My mother had been drinking. She was upset about Mexico, and begged me not to go. Not to go anywhere. Don't ever leave me, she sobbed, clutching at some part of my chest her fingers couldn't quite grasp. I did not make any promises I knew I could not keep. Into the night, I talked to her sad empty fists. I was amazed she could not tell how ridiculously stoned I was. I was amazed that I could carry such a big obvious secret and keep it hidden. For the first time, I became aware how much it was possible to work undercover, to pretend one thing, but really pay attention to a bigger picture. The hash oil buzz had solidified into a harsh vivid clarity that was part cruel and part kind and all knowing.

I was really too stoned to be all knowing, but there I was with my mother, clutching.

Bird charming: age 13

Nowhere did the bird books warn that the family pet, a small hand-raised parrot, might be interested in having sex with you.

The first time it happened, to my mother, it was unclear what exactly the bird was doing. Just being extra cuddly perhaps, and attentive, some wing draping, some squirming around, one or two *Oh my*'s from my mother, and then—it was over. He suddenly pulled himself together and flew away, leaving a spot of evidence behind.

After that, once he'd had a taste, the bird would try to manipulate one of us into a situation where he could "do" his "thing."

On a gross level, his charm consisted of regurgitated seeds, which he'd bring up and offer to the edge of a fingernail. He'd twirl a moist glistening clump, chirping and chatting in a special hoarse sexy voice. Ideally, the finger responded to his overtures. Tapping the flat of a fingernail against his beak excited him greatly. (Otherwise, all his interactions were with mirrors. A finger at least was alive in a way that a reflection could never be.)

Anyway, he'd get all excited, and cover your hand with his wings, and whip his little tail around like a son of a bitch.

Bird Charming was cute and lively, although a bit messy. He'd get off on your hand, managing to keep his own food offering, and leaving behind a spot of white to be wiped off. White, with a speck of blood. Almost always with a spot or little smear of blood marking the white.

The bird's favorites were me and my mother. He experimented with other family members, but went with results.

My mother and I were not interchangeable. We offered variety. We each had our own style of getting him off, but the bird was not always accommodated. He was forced to exercise all his charm. Waves of feathers cresting, he would bob his head and chat me up in his make-out voice. *George is a pretty bird*, he'd say, which (I have to confess) I enjoyed hearing. *George is a prit-tee prit-tee bird.*

The seed offering worked best for my mother. She never failed to be touched by actual presents. She appreciated the gesture. Oh look, he's trying to feed my fingernail. Dirty bird, she'd coo, but wiggled her finger enough to keep him interested, and let him do his thing. She'd *tsk-tsk* and watch soap operas on television, holding her hand away.

Oh you silly bird, she'd fake-criticize. What are you doing? Hurry up and let me get back to my knitting.

My mother in this setting was gentleness itself, and let the bird do most of the work. I had a different style, and rapped smartly up into his beak with a stiffened finger. Mom said, don't hurt him, but the bird loved a finger with a bit of attitude. He became even more cocky. His pupils dilated. His head swelled. He liked it rough, but not too rough. A certain gentle roughness drove him wild. He'd fluff out and scrunch down on the back of your hand and become excited beyond words.

And that would be it.

Once he got going, he could do his little thing and finish off without you, really; he just needed to mount your hand and talk up your cuticle, his little tail going like a curling broom, and it would all be over in no time.

When he was horny he could be a pest. And Bird Charming was horny.

Sometimes, you'd just let him do his thing quick, so he could develop a need for his own space and leave you alone for a while. After he came, he always wanted to go back to his place and be alone in his cage, maybe take a nap, or talk quietly to his mirror-friends.

The Politics of Pride: A Personal Journey

Katherine V. Forrest

For LGBT people of my mid-twentieth century generation, books depicted us with revulsion or pity; films portrayed us in ludicrous, hyper-fervid fantasies of evil; abnormal psychology texts grouped us among the most disturbed of deviates. But somehow, out of this context, we found a way to survive, to find connections, and make a life for ourselves. Out of this context and out of the course of my own life emerged a writer.

My personal journey is not that much different from many of our stories. From as early as age five, I had been falling in love with my female playmates except for those obligatory few tomboy years when I preferred the adventurous neighborhood boys to the uninteresting girls. By the time adolescence brought a drastic change in attitude, I had learned unambiguously that any orientation beyond friendship with my own gender was unacceptable to my parents, peers, and to my church.

So, I would be like everyone else. Match up. Be accepted. No matter what it took. I would successfully run the gauntlet of my peer group and society.

It was a goal so unrelentingly difficult that I spent my late teen years committing every other sin in the book rather than succumb to the one I yearned to commit. That sin might be technically forgivable, but I knew in my depths it would be an irrevocable act, a one-way passage to another place. Like so many self-denying gay people of my generation, I muddied my own life and the lives of anyone who cared about me. Self-hatred did its insidious damage to every relationship, and I marched on to the next one and the next, leaving the wreckage behind and convincing myself that I was really okay, I just needed time, and with a little more maturity I would grow out of this aberration and mature into what was expected of me.

Even after I committed the Big Sin, making that irrevocable passage, and even though I thereafter found women who loved me, and even though I had loving relationships, I remained essentially in the grip of all the early shame and my own powerful homophobia. Until I was forty years old.

I had always wanted to write, and did write—in the same way as I had tried to live my life, the way the world expected me to write. But, at age forty, forcing its way to the surface was a book, unbidden, the book that was mine to write—*Curious Wine*. I have perhaps written better novels in the years since, but none I will ever love more than this book in which I claimed my identity, found my truth, my integrity, my pride, my voice, and my future.

From the perspective of today's open and sexually free lesbian community, it seems astonishing that in 1983—a mere quarter century ago—*Curious Wine* was a breakthrough book for erotic candor. In writing a book that I myself needed and wanted to read, a book that conveyed the passion and beauty of lesbian love and of how very beautiful women are together, I wrote the book that other lesbians wanted to read, and continue to read: *Curious Wine* is one of the most popular lesbian novels of all time, selling as well today as it did in 1983.

Few readers see everything an author puts into a novel, and there are some elements that only the author will probably ever know and understand. *Curious Wine* is universally considered a romantic story without political issues. But my artistic choices were indeed political, and challenged many stereotypes of that day. The two major characters, Diana and Lane, are not adolescents drawn by the mystique of the forbidden; they are thirty-two and thirty-four years old, with considerable sophistication. They are not taken in by any factor having to do with emotional immaturity. Neither woman fits into any mold of psychological dysfunction, nor into the heterosexual mythology of the time that one lesbian was always "the man," nor the belief that women become lesbians because they are unattractive to men—Diana is very attractive, Lane classically beautiful, and they have had positive heterosexual experiences. They are college-educated and professionally successful, their economic independence allowing many options. Out of all these options they choose the most difficult: a life with each other. Unusual for its time, *Curious Wine* also portrays a heterosexual parent who does not reflexively reject his lesbian child. Deeply troubled by Diana's admission, her father, instead of issuing rote condemnation, asks for time to re-examine his assumptions.

I wrote the novel to celebrate not only the beauty of our love but its rightness—and politics is implicit in every line of this "simple" romance.

Around the time that my second novel was published—*Daughters of a Coral Dawn*—I was casting about for the ingredients to fit a concept I vaguely envisioned as "a lesbian life in process." I was already working on a mystery novel with the theme of abuse of power, which I knew would have considerable resonance with a lesbian audience, and it was a theme which, it turned out, would pervade much of my work. I set the novel in the business world, a remarkably under-utilized background in fiction considering that most of us spend a third of our adult lives in offices and cubicles. The murder victim is a tyrannical executive, the suspects are his emotionally and spiritually battered employees. At that time, women were finally moving into the higher echelons of police work, and, realizing that I would need police investigators on the scene, I decided that my investigating detective would be a woman.

And so onto the pages of *Amateur City* stepped homicide detective Kate Delafield of the Los Angeles Police Department: my lesbian life in process. Here was a woman in a high-visibility, high-pressure, and high-stakes profession. An imperfect woman with integrity and decency, around whose very professional and capable shoulders I could swirl the political winds of her increasingly volatile and visible community. And, perhaps most importantly of all, she was a lesbian in the closet who presented the very best-case scenario for anyone arguing the practical necessities of being there. It was a serendipitous meeting of author and character—because who better to explore this woman and this issue than a writer who had spent forty years locked in her own closet?

Over the space of what eventually became a series of eight books so far (the next one will be the last), readers who have followed Kate from the beginning perhaps now understand that this woman of great integrity is at the same time greatly flawed, and the flaw is her rationale for remaining in the closet. She still will not see how it has limited her life and her options, isolated her on the job, removed her from her community, and distanced her from a lover who is increasingly impatient with a partner whose choices and politics diverge so radically from hers. In the most recent of the novels, *Hancock Park*, Kate Delafield finally reaches a crossroads and a collision that's become inevitable.

Between *Curious Wine* and the eight Kate Delafield books, and over the space of fifteen works of fiction, my work has represented the growth of a community, and of a writer. My work has presented in an entertaining format (I trust) many of the issues important to my community. Deeper into this new century in America, except for lesbians who are totally isolated, all of us have grown in political awareness and identity. I'm grateful to have seen these changes in my lifetime, to have chronicled them in my work, to have had a character like Kate Delafield to explore and portray.

The emphasis in my work has been on coming out—the great unfinished business of our community and the great lesson learned from my own lesbian life. Speaking the truth of ourselves is the most important, most empowering step any of us can make to achieve personal dignity, and that any community can make to achieve political stature. The personal is indeed the political, as the LGBT community continues to prove each and every day in each and every one of our lives.

Survey Says

David C. Findlay

In porn, when a stranger looks at you hungrily you know what to expect. It's different in zombie films.

Which of the following traits indicates that a person is a zombie?
  a) Turns automatically toward bright lights
  b) Appears confused when asked about safer sex practices and personal sexual history
  c) Cannot speak
  d) Tries to eat your brain

A couple of years ago I became a mythical creature. The papers said so. Specifically, the papers announced the results of a scientific study in which somebody showed porn to groups of men in two cities. Apparently, very few of the self-described bisexual men in the study got equally hard watching "straight porn" and "gay porn." "Bisexuality," the headlines trumpeted, "is a myth."

Which of the following demonstrates that it's safe to have unprotected sex with someone?
  a) Their limbs don't fall off during foreplay
  b) The sex is non-penetrative; the stickiness happens on their face and hair
  c) They tell you that they're clean
  d) You can tell by looking that they're not Haitian, bisexual, sex-trade workers, or intravenous drug users

I'd love to do a study on that study. Who got to decide that a porn movie was gay or straight? At what point does the improbability of an onscreen fantasy make viewer orientation irrelevant? Did anyone fall asleep, and if so, what did that prove about their preference?

I strive not to be dull to watch, just in case there are cameras present. One of my strategies is to have a lot of public sex. For most of my life I've been doing so by what feels like mostly queer methods, mostly with queer people, in mostly queer space. We've fought to maintain those spaces, sometimes by pushing the boundaries of accepted visible behavior and sometimes by staying carefully within the bounds of expected, accepted appearances. Recently, most of the queer people I'm playing with in public spaces are women.

On January 10, 2007 at about 12:30 p.m. I had excellent Mexican food and a few bottles of dark beer followed by about five hours of public sex at the Metro theater. The Metro is the last of Toronto's big-screen porn theaters. Emptied by competition from the Internet and DVDs, it's been up for sale for years and is now rumored sold. On this sunny Thursday afternoon I found it still open for business, grimy to a point somewhere between decrepitude and pure poetry. I came into this environment on a second date with a shy, smart, and very attractive person whom I met through the wonders of the World Wide Web.

Five hours is a lot of two-story-high pixelated people coming and going on the big screen, and a whole lot of attention two horny people can pay to each other in the tiny seats. Damned cramped little aisles aren't meant for a full grown man to crouch in for the duration of a movie, either, but we were enjoying ourselves.

Which of the following is the most accurate reflection of someone's sexual preference?

    a) The hairstyles of performers in their favorite porn movie
    b) The distribution of bodily fluids in their favorite porn movies

c) The political subtext of their favorite porn movies

d) The environment in which they prefer to watch their favorite porn movies

Our joy earned the attention of our fellow porn enthusiasts early in the program. She and I were working up to an interesting rhythm. Above me, I was hearing her breath accelerate and get louder. I was sensing an impending crescendo for her, and thereafter the chance to depretzelize my limbs. My universe was timeless, dark, wet, and perfect, bounded by her thighs. Her breathing picked up speed again. She tasted like bravery seasoned with sweat. She stroked my bald head. I got a good grip on her leg with my free hand, preparing for a wildish ride. In the way that these moments sometimes do, everything began to blend and blur: her breath, her taste, the distant sounds of the movie, her hand, her warmth … her sudden pause and panicked whisper:

"Stop. Get up here. Now."

I crawled most of the way up her chest before I had to stop, clinching like a punchdrunk middleweight.

Which of the following could interrupt your enjoyment of the movie you are masturbating to?

a) Somebody comes in somebody's face

b) Somebody loses face in public

c) Somebody faces loss

d) Somebody's face falls off

"All of them were surrounding us!"

She sounded worried.

I wasn't ready to turn around. I stayed with my face between her lovely breasts. I saw red and silver with my eyes closed while a susurrus of feet on crusty carpet was drifting away.

"They were here? Up close? Maybe they thought we were hot."

"They were circling around us. Getting closer. Not doing anything, just staring."

I was confused. Her voice still carried a touch of panic.

"If they had their dicks out, if they were enjoying the spectacle, that would have been cool. Very cool, even. I might have come really hard. They were just watching, though. As if they were only half there. Like they weren't really alive. Rude. Creepy. Do you think we should get out of here?"

I remember the day when public movie theaters were a bastion of raw, direct, man-to-man cruising. I wasn't around for much of that era, but I started young and took in what I could. I saw the change as open public spaces gave way to home video and cine-warrens owned by film production/distribution companies. I saw the social skills that flourished in daytime porn theaters all but disappear.

In my teens, sometimes I'd go to the big theaters for a Peewee's Playhouse moment. Reflected light from the screen would be the only illumination, and in the half-blind moments before my eyes adjusted I'd have to try to find a seat. Some men sat alone and were approached and other men did the approaching. I sat alone because I was new and nervous and had no clue about how to craft an approach. I listened. Approaches had to meet the challenges of darkness, probable cultural difference, and the near-certainty that either approached or approacher was operating in their second or third language.

Responses didn't look as complicated. Guys seemed to default to four common categories of reply:

"Yes, please, and may I do you too?"

"No, I'm only into women."

"Yes, but I'm only into women so I'm not going to look at you."

"Yes, but use your hand, and do it slower."

Back at that tail end of the porn theaters' golden age, rarely did

I witness any of the bluster or threat one might expect from men bumping into each other in the dark. I think that means there was something beyond individual horniness going on, some common understandings and some agreement on a common goal. We certainly didn't have a common identity or a shared picture of our preferences.

If there was a similarity, it might have been the scarcity of uncomplicated sexual identities. It's possible I was rare in having a continuity of preference presentation between my life outside and inside the theaters. For some theater patrons, my comfort marked me as not straight enough to be desirable. For most of us, identity didn't seem like the most pressing concern.

Outside the theater, the appearance of heterosexuality was a privilege-laden cloak of invisibility laid upon our shoulders by default in the carelessness of a stranger's gaze. Strangers gay and otherwise were indistinguishable by behavior inside the theater, but this was not gay men's space. It was space carved out in a way that existed before Stonewall, in a way that allowed identity to sit quietly wherever it wanted while the rest of us played.

Which of the following motion-picture genres most accurately portrays middle-class Western adults engaged in a typical process of seeking and getting sex?

   a) Horror films just before the monster shows up

   b) Romance films

   c) Ads for women's deodorant

   d) Mainstream straight porn

There is a difficult moment early in so many horror movies when the protagonists have a glimpse of the threat, consider retreating, and then resume whatever provocative, risky behavior they were engaged in.

After some discussion my date and I went back to playing. She looked up occasionally, licked her lips and grinned—sometimes at me, sometimes at the screen, where the afternoon's hundredth money shot was raining down. This time it was on slender, blond "Olga," in a hotel room somewhere in the Ukraine. She had the on-screen company of a heavyset, fortyish American man who expectorated constantly. Maybe he was trying to compensate for a notable absence of naturally produced or bottled lubricant. Each time he spat, Olga pronounced "Oh yeah!" with identical inflection. She looked expectantly to camera and uttered the same sounds again as the American guy squirted semen on her chin. My date and I shook ourselves and returned attention to each other.

Cut to black.

Which of the following statements is provably false?
  a) Normal bisexual men volunteer to watch porn with metal measuring devices attached to their genitals for the sake of science
  b) Normal straight men touch each other in porn theaters while watching movies featuring men and women touching each other
  c) Normal gay men crave media attention—any media attention
  d) Normal straight porn functions mostly to let male viewers feel as if they are the female performers, surrendering vicariously at the hands of other men

"Do you like coming on people?" my companion asked.

She had shivered and ground against my hand during the closure of the scene with Olga. She looked at me again, still grinning.

"Yes. It isn't central to my sexual universe, but I like it."

She thought about that.

"Do you like coming on people's faces?"

"I do."

She resumed being extremely good to me. I watched, spellbound. The writhing, yelling individuals on screen could not compete with her calm, focused expression, her brush cut spiky in my hand, and her wide eyes looking up from my lap. I tried to have a clearer discussion with her about if, when, and where she wanted me to come. I warned her of incipient torrents. She nodded and smiled, said, "No."

I tried to imagine exactly what she was denying, and what that might mean. I wondered how much longer I could postpone the inevitable. Ahead of us, a man pressed into the crack between the seats, his face almost level with hers.

Behind me the only other vocal person in the entire theater sighed heavily and made slippery noises. The other twenty patrons were silent. Dead silent. From down near the stage at front, one of them started to shuffle up the aisle toward us. His motion was slow and almost painful-looking, as if he'd been seated for months or years and had almost forgotten how to walk, but he didn't pause. My date didn't pause in her ministrations, and we all continued on our respective trajectories.

Which of the following scenarios is most likely to lead to the spread of sexually transmitted infections?

  a) Casual sexual contact where it is prohibited but tacitly allowed while seated on painful, creaky chairs in a public theater

  b) Casual, sandy sexual contact where it is prohibited and alternately punished/ignored while hiding in the undergrowth next to a public beach

  c) Casual sexual contact where it is encouraged while drinking in a bathhouse

  d) Casual sexual contact where there is no regular place, prohibited or otherwise, to meet for any sustained amount of time

Three weeks later, the outcome of that date cleaned up but not forgotten, we found ourselves at Hanlan's Point, where a portion of the beach is legally sanctioned as "clothing-optional." It's now an integrated, family-friendly, edging-toward-commercial space with a still significant but rapidly declining percentage of gay male sunbathers. Tourists and locals vie for patches of sand, titter and gawk, pretend not to be using their cellphone cameras.

We had retired to a quiet space in the dwindling stand of trees just behind the beach, and I was on my knees again. She stood with her back against a tree, trying to ignore mosquitoes and the two fully-dressed guys with golf clubs who were peering through the trees. She came laughing, squirting on my chin and chest. We kissed, packed up, and began to trek to the ferry home.

Decades ago, nudity was illegal here. The whole place was overgrown with a maze of bushes and every bush concealed naked male couples and triads. Occasional police 4x4s came down the beach at eighty mph, hoping to catch nudity or more interesting violations so as to issue the kind of tickets that the accused would rarely choose to contest in court. Once I fought such a ticket and won.

More than once I brought female dates to fuck in the dunes. Cops were rare, and the planes overhead could only watch. The discretion of the regulars who kept to the bushes seemed exaggeratedly cautious. I don't believe that their caution sustained the survival of the beach as a gay space or that our less cautious public play hastened its transformation to a straighter space. There are other axes along which a gathering place can be nudged by its users—toward shared, public pleasure, for instance, or away from revenue generation as the primary measure of a place's value. Such nudgings need the kind of sustained group effort that involves talking to one's neighbor.

At the beach in its gay heyday, I most often encountered young, buff white men who were out to friends and family. With these guys, the quiet negotiations of the theater had become abbreviated even further to a gestural shorthand that rarely needed words. I don't know how their visual signals would fare in a darkened cinema, but these men still have other options. Most of them can pay ten dollars to enter a bathhouse for access to themed, mirrored rooms full of silent guys and loud music. The rooms' themes reference places in which men met for sex in days gone by. We occupy them as if to reanimate (to a dance beat) the dismembered corpse of a half-remembered body. In one of these bathhouses, in one of those rooms, twelve transplanted theater seats are arranged neatly into three rows of four. I'm not there.

Which of the following signals a satisfactory ending?:
   a) All the dirty urban spaces are cleaned up and all the empty urban spaces are filled
   b) The heroine comes in her lover's face and exits stage right
   c) The zombies, sated, kiss and make up
   d) The hero settles on one (exclusive) option and buys another beer
   e) ??

Author's note: Apologies to Chip Delany for mangling some concepts that he has articulated a billion times more clearly; many thanks to him for showing the way(s).

Theories about Bodies and Truth

Sandra Lambert

When I met Lee, he was living as a lesbian. Now, after finding out that he was born intersexed and as a baby underwent no-name, re-cords-lost, sexual reassignment surgery, he is a man.

I believe in bodies. The way people say they believe in their coun-try, religion, the scientific method, or love—that's how I believe in bodies. They are the source. They hold all knowledge. They contain our past, present, and future.

I believe in my body—the size three, baby-soft feet, the polio-altered spine, the sensitivity of my nipples, the place on one hip that always hurts, the breadth of shoulders, the softness of thighs and belly, the seldom seen cuteness of my butt, the age spot on my writing hand, and the fading strength of my arms. Sometimes, in clothes, I'm not happy about how I look. A blouse pulls across the front unattractively, pants never fit right, and this dress looks like a tent. Naked, I'm fabulous.

Behind braces and crutches, within a wheelchair, my body is often an emptiness to the eye of the beholder. I have been left on my own to fill the void of outside regard, to inhabit my body as I please. Set ideas of beauty, of health, of sexiness, and of what a woman or a man looks like, have less of a hold on me. I've heard old women talk of this freedom, but I've had it all my life.

Lee and I have one of those his dog and his girlfriend love me, we share rental movies, I think his band is wonderful, he clears branch-es off my roof after a hurricane and wonders what woman's car was parked all night in my driveway, I keep the dog when they leave town, we like each other a lot relationships. Lee had surgeries. He takes hormones. Why, I wanted to know, wasn't his innate knowledge that he was a man enough for him? Why couldn't he be a man with breasts? I couldn't reconcile being true to yourself with hurting your body with drugs. And surgeries—I've known the horror of those since I was a child. I believe in the rightness of bodies, and Lee was taking actions that, to me, said he thought his was wrong.

The most confusing thing was that from the beginning and every moment since, I've known that Lee is right. I've watched other people, and I've experienced it myself—the excitement and peace of "finding the jewel within," as a friend of mine calls it. I know it when I see it, and (I say this having been an actual one myself) Lee is its poster child.

I'm not confused anymore. This is the part where I articulate my new theory about bodies and truth and give a linear description of its evolution, but I don't have anything like that to offer. What I do have are a series of moments....

His girlfriend and I share a knock, open the door, and yell "it's me" style of entering each other's houses. After Lee moved in with her, I'd often open the door to see him rushing out of the living room because he wasn't fully—I mean *fully*—clothed. But today, soon after his first surgery, I'm driving by the house, and Lee waves for me to stop. He strides down the ramp, shoulders back, no shirt, and the sun gleaming on the curves of his tattoos. I try to be annoyed about the male privilege of shirtlessness, but that's not really what is going on here. Lee walks between the stalks of deep purple sages planted on either side of the ramp, and the flowers shake in reflected beauty.

Another time, I've dropped by, and the refrigerator is pulled away from the wall and tools are scattered over the floor. Lee's girlfriend is interspersing not-always-welcome suggestions to him about what to do next while telling me about her day at work. Lee, stretched flat on the linoleum, fiddles with an electrical outlet. I watch his arms reach and his chest press hard against the bare floor. A fifty-year-old scar on the side of my knee aches in response.

"Hey Lee," I ask, "does that make your scars hurt?" Lee turns his head, his cheek now pressed against the kitchen floor, and looks at me. He says, "What scars?" On my way home, I think about the differences between the loneliness of childhood, scared-every-moment surgeries, and an adult making his own choices.

Lee has quit a job that he's hated for years, and we're having a blow-out "retirement" party in a friend's back yard. He passes around all his old work shirts, and many of us alter them. I cut out the name-tag patch and attach it to an earring. "Lee," in gold machine-embroidered script, dangles against my neck. The bass player in his band wears a work shirt as a skirt, and "Lee" is stretched over her thigh. His girlfriend wears another work shirt as a shirt, unbuttoned to show off her sexy bra. "Lee" curves and bends over one breast. Lee jumps in front of her. He leaps and cavorts and pumps his arms in the air like a happy gorilla. He's wearing the old name patch like a dog tag, and it bounces on his chest. It's July and hot. Sweat shines between his pecs.

I believe in bodies. Whatever their form.

Marriage: Why I Took the Plunge

Daniel Gawthrop

On June 25, 2005, my partner Lune and I stood at the bottom of a lush, green garden in my brother's back yard, joined hands, and exchanged wedding vows in front of seventy-five relatives and close friends.

We weren't exactly making history. On that day, same-sex marriage had been enshrined in British Columbian law for nearly two years. Similar laws had passed in other provinces and progressive US states. The Supreme Court of Canada had affirmed equal marriage rights, and the federal Liberal government led by Paul Martin had followed suit by formally legalizing queer marriage across the country. By the time Lune and I were ready for our own nuptials, the commissioner performing the service had already wed more than 300 same-sex couples. Now it was mainstream.

It's never been a habit of mine to swim with the masses. And, as I stood there with Lune, formally promising to spend the rest of my life with him, part of me could barely stifle a giggle. Only a few years earlier, I had expressed public contempt for the "bourgeois" institution of marriage. Now here I was, getting hitched myself and blowing $7,000 on a catered reception on the tony west side of Bowen Island, British Columbia. How had this happened?

For much of my adult life, marriage had hovered near the bottom of the gay community's hierarchy of liberation priorities, somewhere just above lifetime discount privileges at The Gap. Matrimony was seen not only as a luxury; it was heterosexual mimicry of the worst kind, evidence of a deep insecurity based on an inexplicable tendency to seek acceptance from the straight world by emulating it (*"Look, Ma, I'm monogamous!"*). Marriage was about possession, private property, and power of attorney—not love. It was about bland domesticity, smattered with a disquieting subtext of Christianity. In some circles of the activist community, gays and lesbians who wanted to get married were seen, most charitably, as tiresome hetero wannabes. Squares. Bores. Sell-outs. I didn't argue.

When I first came out and moved to Vancouver in the spring of 1989, marriage was the last thing on my mind. It was the year before the city's socio-political landscape was to change forever with the Gay Games, and I embraced my new life with gusto: joining the *Angles* collective and a gay men's writing group, organizing the ice hockey event for Celebration '90, doing publicity for the AIDS walk, attending art openings and dinner parties, and having as much sex as I could. On the question of marriage, I adopted a stance similar to that of Frank Browning, author of *The Culture of Desire*: "Because homosexuals have resided outside the law," Browning said, "they have invented family forms that respond to late twentieth-century needs, while formulating social and moral codes that provide love, freedom, and fidelity." My "family form" was the community of friends, flings, and lovers with whom I had the most in common.

On December 9, 1992, federal Justice Minister Kim Campbell tabled a long-awaited amendment to the Canadian Human Rights Act that included "sexual orientation" as prohibited grounds for discrimination. One group of activists rained on the parade, blasting Campbell because Bill C-108 also restricted the definition of "marital status" to opposite-sex couples and preserved the traditional definition of "spouse." My reaction was, *Who cares?* I didn't share the outrage, and had trouble spouting the kind of righteous indignation about marriage I had no trouble conjuring up when it came to things like censorship, AIDS funding, and gay-bashing. Queer matrimony seemed too marginal an issue in a time when gay men were still dying from official indifference, when lesbians were fired without cause, and homophobia was still rearing its ugly head in ways that trivialized the injustice of heterosexist marriage law. A few years after the Campbell amendment, in a column for Vancouver's gay newspaper *Xtra! West*, I ridiculed same-sex marriage with an almost smug homosexism. "I think weddings are best left to heterosexuals," I sneered dismissively. "They're so much better at mushy sentiment."

That was the ACT UP stage of my queer consciousness—not uncommon in gay men who emerge from the closet after years of self-repression, but rather prolonged in my case. Coming out, for me, had meant waking up from a coma of Roman Catholic earnestness that had secured my loyalty to good works, the Sunday folk mass and "things spiritual"—but had also kept me like an eunuch until I was twenty-five. Once I abandoned The Faith and set about "catching up for lost time," I took the task rather seriously, gradually developing a sexual appetite that knew no bounds.

By mid-2002, I had more than caught up. For two-and-a-half years, I had been living in Thailand on an almost daily diet of bar and bathhouse flings, my few attempts at long-term commitment fading into memory. I was floating dangerously near a precipice of cynicism, resigned to an eternal love life of aimless addictions, when Lune showed up like an ace paramedic at an accident scene and got my vital signs back.

Given that we were hardly equals—Lune was more than a decade younger, uneducated, and an illegal Burmese migrant worker from Karen State—I'm not sure what it was that convinced me he was marriage material. Perhaps it was a combination of the fact he didn't rush to see me again after our first meeting; that he didn't lie when a visit from another foreign man caused a scheduling conflict; that he paid me back, unsolicited, for money I'd given him; or perhaps that he never said "I love you" until we had both established some kind of foundation for saying so. In retrospect, I think it was the fact that he made me laugh every day we were together that made me want to be with him forever.

Whatever it was, my mind began to fill with images of Lune living in Canada. Once I asked him to come and he said yes, nothing could stop us. Not the Canadian embassy's refusal of a tourist visa when I first tried to bring him home with me; not the Immigration department's tough requirements for partner sponsorship once I was in Vancouver and knew this was the only way he would ever get to Canada; not the bigoted whims of the official in Singapore who handled Lune's application; not the Thai border police, who literally threw up roadblocks every time Lune made his way back to Bangkok from Mae Sot (or the Thai embassy in Vientiane, Laos, which tried to prevent him from re-entering the Kingdom—but clearly overestimated the deterrent effect of the Mekong River, which Lune crossed one night after bribing a fisherman); and hell, not even the long arm of the Burmese junta, the world's most Orwellian police state, which tried to thwart Lune's flight to freedom by requiring him to pay huge "fines" to keep his passport up to date.

It's true that we didn't *need* to get married, in the legal sense, once Lune arrived in Canada. The moment he touched down at YVR and was handed his permanent residency card, he was immediately declared a landed immigrant. So we could have just lived common-law. But given all he had gone through to reunite with me, and given all the notches on our respective bedposts we had tallied before meeting, the words "I do" seemed rather appropriate. *Yes, Lune, I DO promise to stop being such an insatiable slut.... Yes, Daniel, I DO promise not to dump you for a rich, old lawyer the moment those Canadian citizenship papers come through.* Besides which, Lune was a former Baptist, Seventh Day Adventist, and Jehovah's Witness who didn't believe in shacking up. I was a recovering Catholic who, despite his atheism, still didn't believe in divorce. I guess we were destined for marriage.

"Equal" marriage has turned out to be neither the assimilationist sell-out that gay activists feared nor the ruination of society that American evangelicals and the current Canadian Prime Minister Stephen Harper still fear. Full legal rights do not necessarily mandate weddings defined by kitschy décor, "The Wind Beneath My Wings," and bad drunks. Ours turned out to be a rather classy affair. My father, literally leading me down the garden path to "give away" his last unmarried child, showed up looking dapper as ever in a navy blue suit and cream fedora. My fourth eldest brother played ethereal melodies on a wooden harp he had built himself and brought down from Nelson for the occasion. And a Thai chef friend of Lune's donated fruits and vegetables he had artistically transformed into beautiful flowers, including a watermelon with our names carved into it.

Needless to say, I take back what I said about leaving weddings to the straights.

Why I Don't Want to Marry (and Why I Don't Want You to Either)

Joy Parks

I

Lately, whenever the small group of lesbians I know assemble for a potluck dinner or Saturday get-together, the talk is no longer about last night's hockey game or who's seeing whom behind whose back. Now, after the salads are put away and the barbeque is cooling, the talk inevitably turns to marriage. Since I'm one of the few visibly femme women in the group, I get asked for advice on what should be worn, what should be served at dinner, and what flowers should be carried. There seems to be a prevailing belief that my ability to navigate a pair of heels or my firm stance against the wearing of white after Labor Day somehow makes me an automatic expert on all things matrimonial.

I'm polite, I don't make a face, but I find a reason to leave the room, remove myself from the conversation. Sometimes I escort the dog outside, but usually I just retire to the powder room to calm my shaking. I like these women. I don't want to hurt them or embarrass them or belittle their feelings. They're decent, they work hard, they take care of their friends, and they're loyal to their lovers. They seem happy and free, and they grow more comfortable with themselves as the years go by.

Why in the world do they think they need to be married?

II

If one is to go by the mainstream media, we have become a people for whom same-sex marriage is the only issue. By speaking out against it, I risk being considered traitorous. When I point out that it may not be as advantageous as it appears on the surface, or that in the long term it may cause us, as a people, more harm than good, I am shouted down. I am accused of self-hatred, of attempting to hold back progress. I am accused of wanting to send us all back to the closet and, in the next breath, damned for demanding we celebrate our deviance, act out, live outside the norm. I am the ink in the milk, the bad seed, the kind of lesbian who gives nice dykes who just want to settle down a bad name.

III

In 2001, Reverend Brent Hawkes of the Metropolitan Community Church defied Canadian laws against marrying gay couples by evoking the old church tradition of banns, the proclamation of an intended marriage. Once the initial two couples were at the altar and in the news, the courts recognized the illegality of granting one Canadian rights that another didn't have, and eventually—but not easily—same-sex marriage became part of the laws of this land. Oversimplification, yes, but plenty of people will write this story. I don't need to. My story is about how, nearly twenty years prior, on July 23, 1983, I and my then-partner stood in front of Rev. Hawkes for our holy union, the closest thing possible to a wedding at that time. I woke on that summer morning drenched in sweat and unable to function, not from the heat of our walk-up in North Toronto, but because I knew that as a lesbian, participating in this ritual was to turn my back on the person I was fighting to become, the freedom to not need outside validation. *It was the only time in my life I had ever felt I was committing an unnatural act.* I loved her—at the time I thought I would forever—but I knew I didn't need anyone's permission to do so. As I stood in front of the mirror in my white lace wedding dress, I could see the future and it wasn't good. The union was annulled exactly two-and-a-half years later. Some things shouldn't be put in a box and labeled, not unless you're ready to pack them away.

Does that make me a hypocrite? Or does it merely prove that I know of what I speak?

IV

I believe that the fight for legal marriage for gays and lesbians is a symptom of much larger issues. I think it suggests a fear of our own sometimes dark and painful history. That it speaks of a failure of the imagination, an unwillingness to be up to the task of living outside what is expected and safe. It smacks of a desperate need to have our loves sanctioned by someone, anyone. The church, the state, it doesn't matter, we're so needy for validation, we'll take whatever you've got. I'm afraid that we've run out of the courage to stand apart, to celebrate our difference, to embrace the fact that we have survived no matter what the circumstances. I don't want to be "just the same as everyone else," which, from the sound bites surrounding the issues, is apparently our new battle cry. We have always found each other, loved each other, and made homes for each other with no need of their laws and institutions. We have had no rules, no roles, and yet we exist. I fear we will become too dependent on tolerance; that we will cease to be while waiting for someone in authority to tell us that we may.

V

In an interview with *Curve* magazine, novelist Jane Rule was asked about the marriage issue. With her characteristic gruff charm and independent spirit, she replied something to the effect that we in the lesbian and gay community should be helping straight people out of their cages, not getting inside with them. She made it clear that was all she had to say on the subject. My heart sang. Jane Rule was a lesbian activist when you could lose everything by being so. She knows the toll it took to get the state out of our beds and out of our lives.

Why would we risk inviting it back?

VI

I live in a country where same-sex marriage is legal. Despite the occasional bit of political grandstanding, it appears that it will remain so. When the laws were first passed, every news show carried stories about the line-ups of same-sex couples at city halls around the country; every newspaper featured a photo of a middle-aged lesbian couple, dressed in their good clothes, showing their wedding bands or sipping champagne. The first lesbian divorce made front-page headlines. But now, there are no line-ups, no photos, there is no news at all.

I want to ask, "What's next?"

But I'm afraid of the answer.

"You got what you asked for. Now go away."

VII

I came out at fifteen, in 1975. It was International Women's Year and radical lesbian feminism was just starting to tune its voice. In study hall, a much-beloved English teacher would covertly slip me copies of *Lesbian Tide* that she had secreted out of the city. At night, under the covers in my room in my parent's house, I read about this new world where lesbians, women just like me (and there was so much comfort that there *were* women like me) were rejecting convention, were rebelling against what was expected. Dykes were brushing up against the edges of separatism, living their lives outside the patriarchy. Within their relationships with women, they were charting new ground through non-monogamy, communal living, and the idea of a greater community. It was glorious and invigorating and confusing, an evolution forward, an opportunity for transformation, a chance to build lives outside institutions like marriage, which had kept us from our true selves and each other. Admittedly, it wasn't perfect, no revolution is, but it was a revolution, and if it didn't change the world, it changed forever those who were touched by it.

Not the church, and not the state,
women must control their fate.

VIII

If nothing else, the tired prejudices and the old ugliness that have been unearthed in the public discourse that surrounds the same-sex marriage issue should prove to us that in our willingness to tone down our rebellion, to act in ways that would afford us tolerance, we have achieved nothing. Nada. It's time for a change in tactics. We need to be more renegade, not less, we need to celebrate our deviance, not hide it under matching white wedding gowns. We need to regain the power to threaten, to shake the dominant culture's fragile underpinnings to the core. I want us to be fearless once again. I want us to rebel, to resist, to stop knocking on the door, and burn it down instead. We need to understand that "they" need us to be acceptable far more than we need to be accepted. Asking to be "allowed" to marry is about seeking permission. We need to remember that we have never needed anyone's permission to live or love as we chose. By rejecting the "right" to marry, I defy the insinuation that we ever will.

Shirts Versus Skins

Christopher DiRaddo

I can still hear the gruff voice of my high school gym teacher shouting out "Shirts verus skins" across the indoor court. The sharp shriek of his metal whistle stopped our sneakers in their tracks, even though the rubber balls we were using for warm-up would keep bouncing.

There would be a fifty-fifty chance I would end up on the wrong team. In my earliest days of boy-on-boy action, "shirts versus skins" was the simplest way for us kids to know who to pass the ball to. Our teacher, wrapped in light layers of Lycra, would divide us into two teams: one to play in our active wear, the other stripped to the waist. Half the boys would stand around in the cold gymnasium, arms slung around their sunken chests, palms hooked on to their shoulders before the game began. More times than not, I was on this team, my cold, bony, almost bare twelve-year-old body clad only in a pair of small athletic shorts, white tube socks, and runners.

I am part Irish and part Italian, which makes most of me hairy. From the earliest days of my adolescence, when a soft comb of peach fuzz began to grow on my upper lip, I knew I would have issues with body hair. No one else in my class seemed to have sprouted much, and some never would. I was the first in my grade to acquire dark tufts under his arms, the first whose skinny legs were sheathed in a thicket of black wire.

The other boys on the court looked at my developing body with wonder and awe. Generally a remorseless gang of tormentors, they surprisingly said nothing, silent witnesses to my emerging masculinity, perhaps afraid to acknowledge the power of my body's transformation, one that was bringing me a lot closer to manhood than any of them. Yet I wasn't empowered. Watching the other boys take off their clothes in the locker room already had me wondering what team I was on in the first place. I didn't need another reason for them to stare back at me.

The whistle would blow again and the game would begin. I would try to keep up with the other boys but it would prove fruitless. I did not play sports well and my semi-nakedness further hindered my athletic ability. Every time I'd reach for the ball, my arms and legs would unravel to expose the newly forming man underneath, baring the dark growth that had begun to envelop my arms and legs, tease my chest, and swamp my armpits. I could feel the cold air of the gym licking at my skin, making me more keenly aware of my upper body. When I did get the ball I'd try to get rid of it as quickly as possible, keeping it close to me in the meantime, my arms locked with the ball pressed close to my chest, conscious of how vulgar and clumsy my body must have looked to my peers.

The other boys on my team, equally exposed, quickly overcame any initial shyness. They weren't distracted by their own bodies, by their emerging sexuality. They played the game as if their skin was as much a part of their uniform as the rubber was part of the ball. With each lunge and each leap they boldly showed off their bodily bravado.

When the coach blew the whistle one final time and the game was over, I'd quickly pull on my shirt and head into the locker room to change even faster into my day clothes. None of us were made to shower, so the light sweat that had collected on the wisps of my hair would be doused by the cooling fabric of shirts and jeans. For the rest of the day I would sit in class, the odors and memories of the game locked underneath my clothes in some kind of hirsute hothouse, my hair growing in the humid darkness.

Over the years, I would continue to hide my awkward body as much as I could. Even as my friends and classmates began to grow into their own masculinity, I shielded mine, ever more mature than everybody elses, under baggy T-shirts in backyard swimming pools, under long jeans in the sweltering summer. As I got older I even began to try products to get rid of my hair: depilatory creams, wax strips, electric razors. I trimmed, plucked, shaved, and even prayed, all in a vain effort to shape my body into the form that I felt it should be.

I don't remember now when it was that my body no longer felt alien. I began to explore it, first alone, and then with partners. Body shame gave way to hesitant pleasure. The bush on my chest became a garden for the soul, the brush on my arms and legs, a soft spread of protective armor. I began to see how it all suited me, how comfortable I had become in this second skin, and how naked I would feel without it.

I suppose the moment when I realized just how far I had come arrived on a random Thursday night out at a sketchy bar with a couple of my friends. Beers around the table, I noticed a flyer announcing that night's contest: $100 would go to the best (and hairiest) chest in the room. I looked around. *I can take these guys.* Excited at the prospect of excelling at something that required me to take my shirt off, I downed the rest of my beer and headed to the bar to sign up.

It took a lot of nerve for me to stand there that night and invite my peers to judge my body. But friends raucously cheered me on as my name was called. I took the stage and stripped off my shirt. I stood in the harsh spotlight next to a handful of other gay men who, like me, had been blessed with a dense mat of chest hair. We smiled at one another. Only one of us could win, but that didn't matter. This place was so much more companionable than the cold gymnasium of my earlier school days.

What I didn't know back then was that the world we live in as children is not the same as the adult world, and the part of us that we are ashamed of in one is something to celebrate in the other. I won the contest that night just by getting up on the stage.

And today I can honestly say that I am proud of my roots, no matter how dark and thick they are. Without them I would no longer know who I am.

A Lollipop and a Dime

Blaine Marchand

Intergenerational sex has become a sound bite that, like so much in our society, disguises what really happens. News accounts portray, on the one side, boys, now men, as victims and on the other side, men, now elderly, as sadistic demons. What is the truth? Is it always one or the other?

My own interest in this subject is not non-partisan. I had my first sexual experience with an adult when I was eight and then had a relationship with a priest between the ages of twelve and fifteen.

In the first instance, it was a one-time event (let me add, with a stranger) and yet it has remained so vivid. It was near a wooded area where I grew up, not far from Ottawa's infamous cruising spot, Remic Rapids (some things never change). It was a summer's day and I was on my way to swim at "the point," the neighborhood swimming spot on the Ottawa River. For some reason I took his striped overalls and cap to mean he was a garbage man. He said he needed help, offering me a lollipop and a dime if I would oblige.

Although at first I was wary, he finally coaxed me. We went off the road and down a path that led toward the river. As we entered the trail, two teenage boys rode by on bikes in a nearby abandoned lane. He pulled me down to hide. For that moment when we lay side by side, suspense electrified my body. The memory is infused with the sweet smell of earth and grass, the chime of leaves in the trees, the warmth of the sun upon my back like a hand. All of my senses were keenly alive.

We stood up. He asked me to close my eyes and open my mouth while he got out the lollipop. I opened my eyes, saw what he had actually popped into my mouth. I ran away frightened, confused. He called to me. I turned around and glimpsed him holding a dime in his fingers. It radiated with sun. But fear coursed through my body, so I spun around and kept running. All the way to the river, the scene played over and over in my mind.

Through the years, I have wondered why that happened to me. Was it mere coincidence? A fluke of timing? Or, did he see something in me that signaled to him that I would be susceptible, open to suggestion?

When I say it was my first sexual experience with an adult, I phrase it this way because sexual exploration among some children in the neighborhood was a frequent occurrence. Largely instigated each time by one boy, I often wondered where he—the same age as me—had learned to do the things he would suggest. Through our fumbling in the back lanes or behind garages, I learned the pleasure the body gives and takes; how the weight of flesh on flesh is comforting.

I learned, too, of the shame. I remember my mother bathing me, and in the bath we talked about what the man had done to me. She knew because I had, with early male bravado, told friends about the lollipop, laughing at the ugliness of his sucker. One of my friends told his mother, who told mine.

My mother handled the news with calm and clarity. She didn't make me feel ashamed or dirty; that came when my father quizzed me later. But there had been something cleansing in the act of being bathed. It was as if the incident swirled away with the water that went down the drain and was carried back to the river.

I do not condone sex between children and adults. The adult knows what he is doing; it is a relationship based on manipulation. I suspect that in the adult's mind, sex with a child is not really sex—that is what happens between adults. But equally, unless the act is violent, I do not think that it is sex that hurts the child. Rather, it is the mixed messages that wound the child.

Adult men who want sex with boys will coddle the child and appeal to him with whatever they figure will get the child to trust them. They will dote on the boy, offer candy or money as a first act of acceptance. But once the act is over, the adult pushes the child away, giving him conflicting signals. A child does not have the cognitive or experiential capability to understand this push-pull reaction. He has done something to please the adult. Now he is punished for having done it. It sets up a schism, or a divided self within.

Equally, the reaction of parents or anyone who learns of the situation can be equally dangerous and harmful to the child. Why was I comfortable and open with my mother, but uncomfortable with my father's probing? Was it that his role was to be the family disciplinarian? Had I stepped over some line that exists between what is and is not acceptable in male relationships? Step on the line in hopscotch and you are out.

I stood before my father in the back yard, hearing questions but refusing to make sense of them. I avoided his face, concentrated instead on his hands, folding and unfolding in growing impatience at my silence. I noticed his scuffed shoes were a distance from each other. Shuffling from side to side, I kept my lips firmly together. I dragged my runners across the dirt.

Undoubtedly, a part of the problem was our religion—Roman Catholicism, with its line between wrong and right, mortal and venial sin, the holiness of the soul and the evilness of the body, heaven and hell, salvation and condemnation. Tell the truth, never lie.

I repeat: sex between children and adults is wrong. But I will not deny my later love for the man who wore a clerical collar. He was not, as the media or others proscribe, a monster. Rather he was a confused, unhappy, conflicted man who could never accept or be at peace with who he was.

Our relationship lasted but three years. It was much more about affection and discussion than it was about sex, although that did occur. In some moments, ironically, I was cast in the role of the father confessor. As we sat on rocking chairs along the rectory balcony munching caramel candy, he told me about a youthful relationship (although he was careful enough never to hint it was sexual) with one of the actors of *Les Plouffes*, a famous Canadian television comedy in the 1950s. He had wanted to be an actor, but his family wanted him to be a priest.

He was a tangle of emotions and I got caught up in them. This for me has remained the difficult part when I try and understand our relationship, piecing it together like a jigsaw puzzle. He would make promises and break them. He would ask me to spend time with him, then would send me away (as a punishment—for me or him?). He would condemn sexual behavior, yet his voice betrayed prurience. He would touch me, then be repelled by what he had done. He would cry and ask me to forgive him and not to mention it to anyone. One evening, when I was fifteen, he lashed out at me with fury, belittling me, calling me a phony. Even today, there remains a trace of bitterness, like soured milk, about how people you love so openly can be so cruel, driven only by selfishness and need.

The difference between the incidents with the two adults lies partly in my age. At eight, I was confused but largely uncomprehending. At twelve, on the verge of puberty, I was confused about roles and my own yearnings, but conscious of what we were doing. By fifteen, I could read between the lines he fed me, of what others called what we were doing. And the pain of his rejection was excruciating. Faced with all this, I distanced myself from it, as if observing it from some remote plain, from above. It had been a carefully orchestrated relationship. Much like a dance—he led, I followed. I disavowed my heart and the love it held for him. I did so for many years.

Now, when I look back at all this, I do not judge it as damaging me. Yes, it has made me tentative and hesitant about myself and in my relationships with others. But I see I was taught at a young age about the frailties, the peculiarities, the peccadilloes of human nature.

I learned, as all gay men do, whether early or later in life, that there are both joys and sorrows in loving men.

Tribute to a Community of Artists: A Femme Diary

Mary M. Davies

I

It is 1978. I am backstage in the gym at Queen Elizabeth High School, waiting to go on for "Take Back Your Mink." The other Hot Box Girls are milling around in heavy makeup and high-heeled shoes, the rest of the cast in tight dresses and pinstriped suits.

I'm wearing a champagne-colored camisole and teddy, which we all had to buy at Eaton's, all the same, and my sister's high-heeled sandals, also champagne-colored, which she got at a yard sale. The stage manager is holding the mink coats on a rack until just before we go on. They were lent by various rich mothers from the South End, and must be carefully guarded.

I'm sitting apart from everyone because I feel alone. I didn't really know how to put the makeup on, and the other girls got their shoes at real shoe stores and intend to wear them after the show is over. I have no words yet for the way my liking these heels, this lace, feels different and secret. I can't share it with the other girls here. My longings are a nameless ache in my heart.

I have no idea about the future, the years to come of flannel shirts and short hair, of drunken nights and cutting skin, of secret passion that will fester till it can bloom. Of looking and looking for something I can't name, but will surely know when I find it, something that will shine the light on the part of me that craves this silky-lacey fabric on my skin, the way these shoes make my legs feel so long, the exquisite touch of fur on my cheek. Who will help me choose things like this, and who will I want to show them to? No one I know now talks about these things that I thought were secrets.

Our cue. The assistant stage manager, a girl who looks like a boy, comes to line us up. "Hot Box Girls!" she calls in her efficient, no-time-to-lose voice. "All right, good, follow me," she says, and we do, into the wings, where we each slip into a borrowed fur. I don't look to see if she is watching me. Though I'm about to go on stage, I don't yet have any sense of who my audience is.

Part of what I'm looking for is objects of my desire. The other part is reflections of myself. Now, in 1978, my imagination is nowhere near that big yet. But this silk, these heels, this fur, are some kind of glimmer. This is only the beginning.

II

It's 1995. I am reading everything I can get my hands on by and about femmes, which at this point is *The Femme Mystique* and *The Persistent Desire*. I see parts of myself in these stories: being hit on by straight guys, feeling not quite at home in dyke communities of the 1980s.

People are talking about Lipstick Lesbians. We are being feminine-baited with the idea that you can be a lesbian and still be "feminine enough." But this term gets used in a way that negates sexuality and desire, that's all about palatable appearance. I don't feel represented. The people I desire are erased.

I'm looking around. I have wonderful friends, straight women who are silent about sex, gay men who wish my partner were feminine like me, people my other friends call "seventies lesbians" who hate men. I am looking for wider imaginations, new language, community that feels like home.

III

It's 2000. Femme is now a word that gets used in places where I feel at home. Gender Crash has started in Boston. We are writers and performers looking for and making up new language to tell who we are, to tell about our genders and our desires. Someone comes up to the microphone to share a story, a poem, a rant, an explanation, or something they can't explain. The rest of us listen. Then we clap and cheer. This space has been created on purpose and shared by people who need it—space where sexuality, sex, desire, gender identity (specifically trans and genderqueer) can be explored and celebrated. We mean to do this.

There are femmes here, genderqueer boys and girls, trans folks, butches, dykes, fags, people who are embracing and bending and stretching and discarding labels. There are ways to talk about it all. This feels like what I was looking for, what I couldn't name, but surely would know when I found it.

I read a piece I wrote called "Diary of a Comfortable Shoes Femme." I wrote it because I have felt like the wrong kind of femme. High heels hurt my feet. They are like a costume—not in the sense that I feel like someone else when I wear them, but that I only wear them for a very specific audience. I have now been through the years of flannel shirts and short hair, of drunken nights and cutting skin. I am finding a community where I can relax in comfy shoes and lace underthings and have a language to talk about it that other people understand.

IV

It's 2003. I am backstage at a friend's thirtieth birthday celebration show, waiting to go on for my lip-sync performance of "Take Back Your Mink." I have on my costume: black high-heeled sandals, which I bought at Payless Shoes a year and a half ago; black stockings, slip, and camisole, which I wear under my street clothes all the time now. Fake pearls and eyelashes from the Party Store, and half a yard of fake brown fur, which I bought because there are no rich mothers to lend me a real fur coat. And shiny long black gloves. I've worn these things for the wrong audiences before, gotten my heart broken, felt misunderstood.

But tonight's different. I'm waiting for my cue, waiting to surprise a bunch of people who love me, and some who don't know me yet, hamming it up to the only show tune I can really say I know.

The performance before mine is over. Everyone's clapping and cheering. A girl who looks like a boy comes backstage to tell me she's setting up the chair for my number.

"I'll come on when the music starts," I say. She leaves me. I stand up, wrap my fur around my forty-year-old femme shoulders, strut onto the stage to whistles and cheers from people who truly understand the language I'm speaking.

V

It's 2004. There's a book our community made, called *Pinned Down by Pronouns*, full of stories and conversations about the places where gender meets race, class, sexuality, age, physical ability, religion, parenting, addiction, desire. We take it on the road, looking for communities like ours. Nine of us go on a road trip from Boston to Montreal for the Transsexual Day of Pride, perform at Café Esperanza, eat poutine in the gay village and hot souvlaki on St Viateur, and walk in the snow at midnight talking about how we have to write this all down.

It's 2005. The honeymoon's over. This community isn't perfect. Individuals and groups get hurt, feel excluded. Some of us make wrong assumptions, screw up people's pronouns. Femmes get teased or put on pedestals. There is drama and heartbreak. There are pressures to be the "right kind" of fill-in-the-blank. It's all real.

But I keep coming around because of love and because there's a culture of listening. Someone gets up to the microphone to share a story, a poem, a rant, an explanation, or something they can't explain. The rest of us listen. Then we clap and cheer. There is a level of hunger for these stories, this sharing, that I have not found any-where else. We keep coming together.

It's 2006, 2007. Gender Crash is packed every month. There are new people reading and performing every time. We call them Gender Crash Virgins. There are visiting featured performers from Montreal, Vancouver, Toronto, San Francisco, Denver, Georgia, from connections our community has made with others like ours. There's loud clapping and cheering until late on a Thursday night. I am writing this down.

There's a documentary in the works. More people are publishing books. We are keeping track of each other, in it for the long haul. We keep coming together. This is nowhere near the end.

Gay and Tired

Andy Quan

A gym acquaintance, the muscular and defined yet without attitude S., asks me what I'll do for this year's Sydney Gay and Lesbian Mardi Gras. He and his friends, as in previous years, are going as sheep. It seems not a commentary on non-conformity, but simply an aesthetic decision. Lest you think that these are actual sheep costumes, they are not. There is wooly cotton padding around their shorts, sheep's tail, possibly ears, or some padding around the arms, but nothing to obscure a view of their gym-built bodies.

I tell him that I haven't made plans for the parade, but intend to go to the party.

"Have you decided what you're going to wear?"

"Uh, no."

"You're kidding, right?"

It's my eighth Mardi Gras season in Australia, following a few years in Europe, after gay student activism in Canada. I'm in my late thirties. I've almost stopped reading the gay community newspapers, but can't help glancing over the letters to the editor section. There are the same tired debates after so many years on: the use of the word "queer," women-only dance spaces, the commercialization and co-optation of a gay and lesbian movement. I can't believe that the rainbow flag is still in use, that the inaccurate ten percent figure is still in currency, the ways that identity politics from the eighties and nineties still resurface. I rolled my eyes at the program for the gay and lesbian film festival this year. Nearly every film aimed at gay men featured "buff," "handsome," "muscular," and "gorgeous" protagonists. But neither do I champion those who declaim that the gay scene as superficial and commercial, lacking in community spirit; I find these people humorless, and dated.

But let me tell you how gay I was.

I was a sensitive, musical outsider in high school, bad at sports, uninterested sexually in girls, unwilling to pretend to be. Without ever having a sexual experience with another person, I came out to a close girlfriend at sixteen. I saw it as a duty to come out to anyone I was close to in college. It was not only a way to build intimacy with friends; I felt charged by seeing their prejudices challenged and fall. I believed I was changing the world.

In university, I continued my mission, coming out to most people I befriended. I came out to my parents, which allowed me to feel really free to embark on my chosen path as a gay activist. I finally had sex. It was mediocre and didn't really change my outlook that sexuality was more about politics than any physical act. I wrote an article in the university newspaper about being gay and signed my name to it.

In my second of three years at university, I carried on the charge. I didn't understand why gay men and lesbians, in our small university town, didn't participate together in community events, so I called for a potluck dinner to discuss the issue. The older gay men and lesbians in town humored me. We all ate vegetarian casseroles and they politely informed me that gay men and lesbians didn't necessarily need to hang out together, and it didn't mean that they didn't get along.

I started calling myself "queer," as it was becoming the fashion, and I thought that it broke down the old categories and political affiliations. I organized, fundraised, and mobilized an entire week of the first Bisexual, Gay, Lesbian Days (BGLAD) at our university with discussions, a cabaret, literary events, a dance, and more.

Looking back, I am amazed at my confidence, skills, and fearlessness at the time.

In my last year of university, I wrote a short story that would be published in Canada's first anthology of gay writing. This would eventually lead to the publication of a book of stories about being gay, coming out, and about being gay and Asian; a poetry book with gay themes, and some years after, a book of gay erotica.

. I did my master's degree in politics, focusing on gay and lesbian topics, with no idea if this could lead to a career, but I figured I might as well try. My first job out of university was as the coordinator for the International Lesbian and Gay Association in Brussels. My family expressed some apprehension that my business card would state "professional homosexual." For two years, I traveled the world, meeting with gay and lesbian activists in countries and continents.

When I moved to London, I applied for more work in gay and lesbian activism, and got hired instead to work for a gay men's HIV prevention agency. Many nights and days were spent in gay bars, surrounded by gay men, living a very gay life in London. I learned about fashion and went to musicals.

I moved to Australia and was hired by the national AIDS organization to do international work. As active as in London, I joined the gay and lesbian choir, gay sports teams, and went to Sydney dance parties. I became a board member for the Sydney Gay and Lesbian Mardi Gras, and trained for and competed in the Sydney Gay Games in 2002.

I was über-gay: gay at work, gay at play, gay on three continents. In the midst of working for Mardi Gras, I'd hear cynical community members say how "over" they were of the "gay community," of Mardi Gras, of being gay itself. But I could never imagine how you wouldn't want to quietly or loudly state your sexuality, participate in some way in a gay event, wouldn't want to change the world, just a little bit for the better.

When I saw the call for essays for this anthology asking what it's like to be gay in 2007, I thought: tired. I've run out of steam and enthusiasm. I am over it. I don't volunteer or belong to any gay group, am tired of the gay bars, and have nearly stopped going to dance parties. I stopped calling myself an activist many years ago.

Some of my friends blame it on age. We settle down, buy property, some have children. But I've met many in my time who remained committed gay and lesbian activists their whole lives, have older friends who remain engaged year after year, and Sydney has a particularly amazing breed of older gay men who have the ability to dance all night, party after party, with no signs of slowing down.

There are reasons for my cynicism and disengagement. Mardi Gras burned me out: I was on the board of an organization that went bankrupt (before a new, leaner one emerged from the ashes). I tend to not do the same activities year after year, but have somehow run out of gay community issues that interest me. And I have a gorgeous boyfriend who is uninterested in the gay scene.

As a professional homosexual now for well over a decade, most of my friends are gay men. I've been surrounded by fellow homosexuals, or at least supportive and progressive straight friends, for as long as I can remember, shielded and cushioned from mainstream intolerances.

My work has also done a turn. International and regional involvement is now leading me away from working only with gay men to dealing with straight men and women, drug users, and sex workers.

I find myself quiet these days, focusing on my own life rather than on a real or imagined gay community. One of my biggest pleasures is watching how my collection of succulents thrives in the Australian sun and heat. Now I'm obsessed not with gay politics, sex, or the "scene," but with my plants.

When I venture out, acquaintances ask, "Where have you been?" Dissonant to my daily life, I'm viewed by many friends as someone who is still fully in the middle of gay life and community, with a packed social and volunteer schedule.

However, I am perplexed. Rationally, I can trace my disconnection with gay politics and community, seeing a trajectory of someone who started out as a young activist and is now, many years later, stepping away. Yes, I burned out, but didn't expect it to be permanent.

I certainly don't begrudge anyone who is involved in gay community development or a literary exploration of who we are as men-loving-men in this new century, it's just that I can't relate anymore. Which is strange, since with the relentless history outlined above, I should empathize, or at least be compassionate. I shouldn't have this distaste, this wrinkling of my nose, this shaking-head sigh-of-the soul.

How did I get from over the rainbow to simply over it?

Not Getting Killed, With Kindness

S. Bear Bergman

This morning, as I was getting a cup of coffee from a café around the corner, someone asked me whether I was raised in this country. Now, I am sometimes asked what planet I'm from, or even whether I was born in a barn, but this question hasn't come up much. I replied that I was, and wondered why she'd asked. My English is unaccented, my general comportment doesn't seem to suggest otherwise; I wasn't listening to French-language hip-hop on my iPod. She said, with some surprise, that she'd wondered because I was so polite, which she does not associate with Americans. Nodding and grinning, I thanked her for the compliment and did what I usually do in such situations: I shrugged and said, "I was raised right."

That's true, but it's a half-truth. It is true that I was raised by parents who, whatever their strengths or faults may have been, placed a very high premium on being courteous and friendly. They taught me to say, "May I please," as though it were a single word, and to say thank you early and often. I learned by example that taking the time to say good morning, to inquire how someone's day is progressing, and to actually listen to the answer, all go a long way toward making one's world a nicer place in which to live. And I internalized a basic understanding of the concept that one gives respect in order to get respect; that it is the height of self-centeredness to assume that anyone will treat me respectfully if I don't treat them in the same way, and that this is true for anyone I encounter in my life, no matter what social status that person's job might seem to confer upon hir. That, in fact, those distinctions are themselves at the heart of American-style rudeness—the idea that the person who makes me a cup of coffee does not deserve to be called Sir and thanked politely as much as the university president who is about to decide if I get a gig or not.

I wish I could say that I have continued practicing politeness as it was taught to me solely out of a deep sense of respect for all other people until they prove themselves otherwise. I would like to be a person who, for no other reason than from a whole-hearted place of honoring the divinity in all beings, treats everyone around me exactly as I believe ze (and all of us) deserves. I'd like to say it, but it isn't quite true. I have to confess to an ulterior motive. If I'm being honest, the truth is that I am courteous and friendly to everyone I meet, or at least that I try to be, because I want them to like me *before* they notice what a freak I am and try to punish me for it.

I recognize that, on the page, this sounds like hyperbole, and in some ways it is. I do not in general feel myself to be in any immediate danger of being smacked around by the receptionist at my doctor's office or beat up by an associate professor of modern literature (though the receptionist at my shrink's office, Trish, is a no-nonsense Southern girl who could clearly lay the smackdown if she cared to). But I never trust myself to make such judgments, and so I make the decision to exercise my particular brand of nice-boy courtesy in all situations.

Also, there are other considerations, gradations between completely accepting and hiding-a-baseball-bat-behind-his-back. The ways of punishment can be so subtle I never know about them, never know what I could have had or done if I hadn't been so threatening to look at. What visibly outlaw person has never been sweetly told that the job was filled, the apartment was rented, the manager was out for the day; that no substitutions were allowed, that *all bags must be checked*, that the thirty-four dollar fee still applied even for a seventeen-cent overdraft? I don't know any. We all pay a price for looking different in any way—from my thirteen-year-old niece the goth princess whose typing teacher sent her to the disciplinary office the day she appeared at school with pink hair, to my former students, elite-level student-athletes in the basketball program whose great size and black skin were so anomalous in our smallish New England town that bank clerks literally played a passive-aggressive game of Not-It in order to avoid having to help them. It was in talking with them about their experiences in the public eye that I started to recognize how much my reflexive politeness and gregarious ability to make a few minutes of social chat with nearly anyone had smoothed my way: I eventually escorted my students to my local bank branch and introduced them to the three tellers with whom I was acquainted from my own visits there, and they had no problems after that. They, too, had moved from Those People to someone individual and knowable.

As someone who moves through the world being visibly queer, visibly beyond the bounds of the traditional gender binary, being someone individual and knowable is one of the most powerful tools I have. I am aware that I am always—whether I want to be or not—an ambassador for my people. At the very least, I am aware that this is always a possibility. And it is a possibility I take seriously. If someone is encountering a queer person, or a readably transgendered person, for the first or even the tenth time, I would like that person to remember me as being, really, perfectly all right. Not freakish or lecherous or miserable or rude or anything but moving easily in my world, giving respect and hoping to receive it in return.

In the best moments, a brief conversation gives me a chance to close the gaps caused by ignorance a little further and make pleasant, small-talky conversation about the weather or the dog or some minor local event. Something that further underscores the idea that although some parts of my life are and will continue to be radically different from theirs—and I am not a proponent of the We're Just Like You Except For What We Do In Bed philosophy—it is nonetheless true that in some ways our lives are not always all that dis-similar. I, too, walk my dog and worry about the consistency of his poop—even if I may share my dog with my queer femme ex-partner who maintains a separate household, which is next door to her best friend who is my former lover and owned boy and also a transsexual to boot. I, too, struggle to remain calm and good-natured while mak-ing alternate arrangements to compensate for air travel delays—even if I am flying to Milwaukee to perform the queer, transgendered, Jewish solo theater piece which is my sole source of income, and the major source of my consternation is coordinating airport pickup for my lover from Pittsburgh who is flying in separately and meeting me at the airport (and is also a transsexual to boot).

I do not always reveal these conditions explicitly (though I have certainly been known to), but I tend to think that they are assumed, if not specifically then generally. Your average heterosexual, Chris-tian mother of three is probably not looking at me and assuming that our lives are full of points of intersection. And let's face it—we're all wary of what we don't know or don't understand. So my working theory is that whatever opportunity I have to close that gap a little bit is a way of activism, as valid as the work I do standing up and lec-turing about gender-y things and probably, in the final analysis, with a higher success rate. I'm trying to demystify queers and transfolk, in both cases, trying to be approachable and basically regular, not afraid to laugh at myself and not afraid to answer hard questions, but also just as glad to sit and talk about the Designated Hitter rule or whether *Law & Order: SVU* is better than the original *Law & Order* series. If I'm going to be someone's introduction to GLBT folks in any kind of setting (and I assure you that there are people who shudder miserably at that idea), I want to use the opportunity to be someone they can like even though some things in our lives are very, very different. I want to move us from Those People to "that person I always see walking his dog who lets my daughter give it treats," or "that person who gave me the name of that great Thai restaurant in Saint Louis." I will happily settle, any day, for "I don't know, that transgender came and talked to our class, and he or she or whatever didn't seem so weird."

But the ways of gender are fickle, and on some days I become aware of the fact that I am not being read as queer or gender-transgressive but as a perfectly ordinary boy, white and at-least-middle-class and ostensibly heterosexual in my jeans and boots. Truth be told, I'm always tempted by those opportunities. It would be so easy to slouch, scowl, mumble "gimme a turkey sammich on rye," let doors bang shut behind me. I could spit and swear and jerk my chin to indicate what I want without even saying a word, certainly not please or, at any further stage, thank you. Not only would it be easy, it would probably help me to continue being read as a boy, as my reflexive politeness in those moments is in fact the most transgressive thing about me.

(I should point out here that this is true especially in the Northeast, where I live, and where a certain crankiness is the default position. In the Southeast, where some kinds of politeness—even if they are rigidly stratified by race and class—are much more common, my courtesy when I am read as a man isn't transgressive at all. In fact, it serves to reinforce that gender attribution. Absolutely nothing says Man, apparently, like fingering the brim of one's cowboy hat in a tipping gesture to a woman and her young daughter, saying first "Ma'am," and then, with a different smile, "Miss.")

This is especially true when that politeness crosses class and race lines. As unusual as it may be for me to address someone working in the service industry as Ma'am when I'm being seen as a transgressively-gendered, female-bodied person, it seems to be even more of a shock to people when the mid-twenties white boy I sometimes am does it. This may be the most gender-transgressive thing I ever get to do—perform the possibility that men can be courteous and friendly in a culture that allows, and in fact expects, its men to be rude and disconnected. So when I take the time to politely inquire how someone is feeling today, or comment sympathetically on a crying two-year-old being half-past naptime, or wait patiently for an elder to pet and admire my dog, I am having almost the reverse experience. These are things that the world expects from women (though I won't speculate here about why) and when I perform them it calls my masculinity and my motives into question immediately. If men don't do such things, why am I doing them? I become, quite against my will, an outlaw again.

Very occasionally, but most gratifyingly, it earns me a heady dose of approbation from a woman nearby. Part of that gratification is about being approved of, of course, but the rest is my sense of pleasure at having created or reinforced or expanded in someone's world the possibility that men can be engaged and attentive and kind. All too often I feel as though the heterosexual women in my world are settling for only a small fraction of what they want, because they believe that they cannot have anything else. Concurrently, I often see the heterosexual men in my life being only a small fraction of what they are, because they have internalized the message that they cannot *be* anything else. It's a great pleasure to imagine that while I'm out being the most polite tranny ever to step a booted foot in my local Dunkin' Donuts franchise, I may also be read as a place on the landscape of masculinity where a sturdy boy in jeans and boots can also hold a baby, both expertly and with joy (and the nice smiles from girls are a lovely bonus).

I enjoy it, either way. I enjoy having the chance to transgress in ways that are welcoming rather than alienating, and I enjoy the opportunities that learning from my parents' example has given me to maybe make some small slice of change. I enjoy knowing the names of my bank teller's three children and keeping rough track of the oldest girl's win/loss record (she's a three-season athlete with a summer swim team to boot and is therefore perpetually winning or losing at something). I like teasing my pharmacist about his taste in neckties and talking about singer-songwriters with my pharmacy tech. I like telling stories to children in airport waiting lounges and passing the time with the other poor souls consigned to waiting on a long line with me. It keeps me engaged and connected with my world, and they with me—with my big fat genderfucking self, helpfully producing an extra pen and smiling kindly. Hi, I'm your friendly neighborhood outlaw. Welcome?

Wild Nights

Simon Sheppard

O, San Francisco, city of horny ghosts....

Nowadays, when I sneak a sidelong glance at my reflection in some shop window, I see someone rapidly approaching "just this side of elderly." But Junior, t'wasn't always this way. There was a time when, heading out for an evening's debauch, I'd check myself out and a hungry young reflection stared back.

Nobody likes a sentimental old fool, I suppose. And nostalgia, as the saying goes, ain't what it used to be. But let me tell you (anyway) that yes, it was good to be young and horny way back in the 1970s—before gentrification, before HIV. Before I became, maybe, jaded. Before I lost my hair.

I was a mere stripling then, and temporal distance lends enchantment; even the Strand, a surely vile movie theater where junkies blew each other in the balcony, seems wreathed in a certain glamour now. But I honestly think it's true: on the gritty streets of San Francisco bloomed a garden of earthly delights, a cock-filled cornucopia redolent of Weimar at its wildest. Ah, those were indeed the days.

And the nights.

I can still recall the feelings of anticipation as I alighted from the Muni bus and headed down some dimly lit street in what was then still a rather industrial part of the city, a neighborhood where faggots and funkiness had not yet been supplanted by het fashionistas strutting their stuff at bridge-and-tunnel *boîtes*. Heading down the sidewalk toward expected stand-up sex, humming Van Morrison's "Wild Night" to myself, I felt so very naughty, so much more sleazily mature than I'd been when I first moved to San Francisco and settled into a gay hippie commune not far from Golden Gate Park—a delightfully drug-soaked place where I rather successfully kicked over the traces of my well-behaved middle-class upbringing.

After dark, you see, lust ran wild at wide-open San Francisco's sex bars.

As someone who'd come of age before Stonewall, back in the dear, dead days of repression, I—like many of my generation—headed out from suburbia to land on the wilder shores of San Francisco. Kid, meet Candy Store. Candy Store, Kid.

Back then I was, in my peculiarly jaded way, innocent ... or at least inhibited. There were scenes where I never set foot: The Cauldron, where "water sports" had nothing to do with surfing; The Slot, where men fisted each other, a pursuit that seemed so anatomically improbable that when I first heard about it, I dismissed it as an urban myth; and the Catacombs, a dungeon so depraved, it was whispered, that The Slot was a convent by comparison.

Yes, heavy kink was beyond my ken. I did, however, patronize a few of the more mundane penis-palaces. I got down on my knees in the misty precincts of the Ritch Street Baths' tiled steamroom, thrusting my tongue into the nether regions of a half-seen muscle-hunk, thereby contracting a positively gruesome case of shigellosis (though not even that erased my taste for rimming). The Bulldog Baths, down on Turk Street in the seamy Tenderloin, featured—if memory serves—the cab of a semi truck plunked down, shining headlights and all, in the middle of a rather butch orgy room, as well as a two-story cellblock, a novelly transgressive *mise en scène* for the same old sodomy.

Still, the bathhouses, however fabulous, however hot the action (and who can ever forget the sight of that famous fister with his arm sunk improbably deep into another man, only to pull it out and reveal he was an amputee?) ran, for all their sometimes-deluxe and always lust-filled ambience, second-place in my affections to San Francisco's infamous sex bars.

If 18th and Castro was the intersection of a burgeoning queer community, the town's throbbing libido was based a little lower down, south of Market Street, south of The Slot. Down on Folsom Street, where the boys' backroom bars were.

In those days, before the Internet made getting laid as potentially easy as ordering pizza for delivery, a night at the backroom bars was perhaps the simplest, safest path to getting one's rocks more-or-less off. And, unlike going to the baths, stopping by a bar for a blow was an impromptu, low-commitment affair; the borderline between a beer at the pub and public sex was permeable indeed.

Okay, I still wasn't nearly as rakish as I thought I was. Yes, I went to the weekly slave auctions at the Arena bar, but mostly to see leather columnist Mister Marcus fling embarrassing questions at near-naked contestants who, when commanded to, readily bent over to display their well-used holes. I had very little idea, though, of what actually went on once the slaves were taken home by the masters who'd successfully bid for them; it would be another decade or two till I learned to swing a flogger and properly degrade tied-up bottomboys. My loss.

I know I hung out at the Hungry Hole, and I'm sure I swallowed gallons of what porn writer Dirk Vanden dubbed "someone's unborn children," but I'll be damned if I remember a single thing about the place. I do vividly recall the back room at Folsom Prison, even though it was pitch black, save for a single dim red bulb somewhere ceiling-ward. That was a venue for venery at its most anonymous, where touch, taste, and smell were all you had to go on. On a good night, bounties of sweaty flesh—indistinguishable as its owners might have been in that Stygian, popper-infused gloom—fused the transcendent and the trashy and the true.

Best of all, though, was the Boot Camp, where the back room

was in fact in the front room, an orgiastic area partitioned off from the bar by nothing more than a few oil drums. I still remember—or at least *think* I remember, which is pretty much the same thing, really—one stand-up fuck, my bottomboy perched on a bench while I plowed away, as one of the breakthrough booty moments of my life. *Can this really be,* I'm sure my stoned mind mused, *the same nice Jewish boy who wanted to be a pharmacist when he grew up?*

If I'm going to get honest with myself, I'll have to fess up that I've wasted an uncountable number of hours in the pursuit of more-or-less random orgasms. Sure, I was looking for love—a love I was shortly to find in an enduring, endearingly open relationship that is, I'm thrilled to note, still going strong. But that search for affection didn't preclude the call of those wild nights, that quest for meaningless, objectified, endlessly lovely male-to-male (to-male-to-male-to-male, sometimes) sex. Because San Francisco was, as it had always been, about adventure, possibility, the gilded bacchanal. Or at least so the myth goes.

And then came the crash, one of the greatest health crises in the history of humankind. Okay, nobody saw it coming. But even if parties weren't made to last, this particular orgy wound down especially quickly and brutally, with a sickening viral thud.

The butch boys and fabulous fisters started dropping like flies. Folsom Street became a ghost town, Castro Street an outpatient ward. Larry Kramer kvetched at us. Homocon Andrew Sullivan castigated us for being immature and irresponsible, even while he was secretly cruising for unprotected sex. We were goaded to disavow sex, drugs, and rock and roll, unless they were, respectively: in the context of a committed relationship; Viagra; and the Clash's soundtrack to a Jaguar ad.

In the bedraggled City by the Bay, wild sex took a decided nosedive. One by one—their clientele gone or going—the backroom bars closed down. The walking wounded of Castro Street served as a *memento mori*: Not only silence equaled death. Sex did, too.

And there followed, for around a decade, a fallow decade of fear. Yes, I was in that amazing open relationship. But I spent much of my late thirties in sexual retreat, or so it seems to me now. And by the time improved treatments and revived sluttishness appeared on the scene, I was shuffling off to middle age.

Still, I was one of the lucky ones.

I survived.

Now the Strand stands shuttered on Market Street, awaiting the wrecking ball. A discount supermarket has been built on the site of Folsom Prison, while biker bar Black and Blue's former home now houses, chromatically enough, a paint store. Folsom Street Barracks bathhouse, destroyed in a massive 1981 fire, has been replaced by a het-yuppie bar serving microbrewery beers. And where the Boot Camp reigned, there's now a Chinese restaurant. At the site of one erstwhile glory-hole palace, there stands the chastely welcoming GLBT Community Center, apparently unhaunted despite being built over an orgasms' graveyard. And me? I'm eligible for AARP.

But hey, it's no use crying over spilled sperm. Some sage pointed out that the very best rock and roll was made when you were eighteen—no matter when you were born. Nope, things aren't what they used to be. And they never were. Still, I can't help but wonder whether in some globally warmed future, some aging pornographer will look back on the Arctic Monkeys and cruising Craigslist with the same unforgivably sloppy sentimentality I reserve for the Velvet Underground and wild nights at the Boot Camp.

I know, I know. The struggle for queer liberation comes down to much more than a furtive blowjob in the dark. Of course, of course. And times change. New HIV treatments have brought some of us, like lecherous Lazaruses, up from the brink of the grave and back down on our knees. Folsom, despite its annual SM street fair, may be a pale shadow of its former raunchy self, but the Castro is vibrant again, even if there's a Pottery Barn hovering above its now-unaffordable precincts. Guys still gather for group fucks at places ranging from the Citadel to the Faerie House. And if barebacking and crystal meth are inviting the Angel of Death to stick around for a while, if desperate men still search for love and find ashes instead, if an endless quest—*my* endless quest—for penis can be, in point of fact, rather problematical ... well, there have been quite enough threnodies, thank you very much. Too many, in fact.

And if many, perhaps most of the men I sucked off at the Hungry Hole are dead now, if I can't even remember their dicks, much less their names, well, in the immortal words of the Little Sparrow, "*Non, je ne regrette rien.*" Or nearly *rien.*

In my more maudlin moments, I have to face the fact that my salad days have withered, leaving a scummy mess at the bottom of the metaphorical refrigerator drawer. But better penis than pathos, says I. And if I'm too retro to forswear sluttishness, if I'm selfish for preferring to suck cock rather than raise kids ... well, take pity on the queer quirks of an aging homo. I refuse to be an apostate to the animal faith of cock. Because an hour ago, a miraculously beautiful man I met via Craigslist walked out of my apartment, leaving behind the taste of his sperm on my tongue. And because, even now, even at the very moment you're reading this sentence, somewhere or other in San Francisco, two men who have just met are naked before each other, erect, and for one long orgasmic moment, everything is, for them, joyful and beautiful and right.

Same as it was at the Boot Camp on some long-ago dark, wild night.

Every Street Has Its Girl

Bonnie J. Morris

My journal and I go out for a walk on a fine October night when the dry leaves look, sound, and smell so great, in perfect sensory trinity. Leaf, leaf, making shapes on paper and sidewalk, a Javanese puppet show of foliage. The many side streets are silent, except for dogwalkers and catering vans; the dogs and gourmands come together at the Bistro Du Coin, which used to be Food For Thought, now offering a dog bowl full of water outside for parked pets. Some kind genius has installed a park bench at the foot of the stone stairs at 22nd and Decatur Street, just below the weather-stained, trickling fountain. This should be my album cover photo, a street where I've worked, loved, prayed, made out in a parked car steaming up its windows. This is all I really want out of life: steamed up windows, a writing environment with lovers in it, silhouetted against some sort of romantic background. If all these scenes of my time in DC were on video, each landmark would be paused: look, remember. Press the pause button and reflect where I have been.

My Washington is Dupont Circle, and I live on Connecticut Avenue, at the top of the hill of our little Beltway Bohemia. I can roll out of bed and down into the great gay mix, past Lambda Rising Bookstore with my own books in the window, over to 17th Street and the bars, coffeehouses, and cozy restaurants of the tribe. Everyone cruises and falls in love here, gay and straight. Read Matches in the back pages of *City Paper* and you'll see the local themes: *You were on U Street in a purple wig. I saw you at the Drag race; you were the little golden angel with pasties and a g-string. Connecticut Avenue: white fur hat and red bike; you were northbound. Coffee?*

I sit in cafés bedecked with rainbow flags, read articles in *The Washington Post* or the *Blade* about the gay civil rights bills being debated before Congress—new statutes that will either limit or expand my latitude as a citizen, woman, dyke, Washingtonian. Ah, but living in the District, I have no electoral representative. Yet I enjoy human rights protections my pals across the Potomac in Virginia certainly don't have. When I ride Metro into northern Virginia to visit one ex-lover, instantly I'm a felon, a homo who eats girls.

My lesbian youth may be behind me now, but here in DC it creeps up on me and taps me on the shoulder, every night. These are the streets where I came out at eighteen, and now in early middle age I can still find my way from landmark to landmark of reckless, inane love. That love of girls, of women, was built upon each corner, traffic circle, curbstone, at restaurants that came and went, at movie theaters that opened and shut like clams, while buildings fell and loomed, and presidents thumbed their noses at gay rights. I live in a map of memories, stretching from Montgomery County to the Capitol steps, Metro stops and nightclubs, parks and stages, and I haven't ceased to add to foolish love. I still flirt with everyone, still find the girl in the neighborhood, the neighborhood in the girl. When I fall in love with someone, I fall under her spell like a petal blown across a pond's surface—skim, wilt, drift, drown, spin.

Cartography: I live on Connecticut Avenue now, but Wisconsin Avenue was the ribbon of my raucous lesbian youth. Here is the drive-through; select your music, please: the Roches, Genesis, the Police, Cheap Trick, Blondie. Start at the Bethesda library, where I furtively checked out *Rubyfruit Jungle* at sixteen, and everything else lesbian in the 301 mark of the Dewey Decimal system. Drive on to Booeymonger's, across from Mazza Gallerie, Booey's where I took every girl I liked in the college years, even the professor I was dating; a café still vibrant and in bloom, where I can press pause and say: I have eaten at every table in that place. Onward up Wisconsin to the movie theaters, to restaurants where I ate with my professor, to Count's Western store where I bought my butchy painter's pants when I was in ninth grade; to a bar where someone kissed me on the mouth, and at the top of the hill to where the Serbian Crown was once, where I took my college lover the night I found I had won a full scholarship to grad school.

Down the hill to Tenley, where it all really happened when I was coming out: Marian Hall, the night I made love to a woman for the first time; Armand's Pizza, where I took another lover the night I graduated; then the core magic block across from Sidwell: the Home Mortgage Association parking lot where I kissed my first girl. Down Wisconsin farther, onward, go: to the left, Macomb Street, where I parked and kissed some more; cross Massachusetts, and shoot down into Georgetown, past the old 9:30 Club where Betty used to play, and the Samurai Sushi-Ko where I've eaten with two loves, and then Wisconsin ends at M, the old Key Theater gone now, but that's where we all dressed up and saw *The Rocky Horror Picture Show* over and over. Olsson's Records, where I dreamily bought Police albums the day after I first slept with a woman, where I bought the Police single "Don't Stand So Close to Me" because it was about a student-teacher affair and I was dating my dance professor; finally, down, down, down to the old Bayou nightclub where I went to my very first two women's music concerts, Holly Near with a sign language interpreter, and Cris Williamson with June Millington and Jackie Robbins. Any farther down Wisconsin and you land in the canal, the canal that stretches all the way back to my family's old house in Bethesda, the canal where I held my best friend's hand on ninth grade afternoons.

Wisconsin Avenue is Oz. But every street has its girl. If I had an airplane, a helicopter, an aerial overview, a map with star-shaped pins to stick in DC, little women's symbols flickering *here, here,* everywhere I kissed or loved somebody, I would see: I have lived well.

I am a cheerful, healthy lesbian on the loose in America's capital. I was fourteen the first year my family lived here, and fourteen when I *knew*, and first told girls that I loved them, held them close; and now I'm forty-five, the numerals a football score: 14-45. And the game's been good to me; I was a very old fourteen and am now a disgracefully playful forty-five, and a great deal happened in between, here in the Potomac's front yard. Love is great with cherry blossoms on it, even while mere yards away Jerry Falwell, Pat Buchanan, and the Family Research Council are conspiring to ban nice homos from America. DC is packed with homophobes, but when prominent "ex-gays" wig out and return to cruising, they end up in *our* bars. And everyone in dyke DC has had that bizarre experience of meeting someone cute at a barbecue and finding out she's Pentagon, and closeted. Everyone asks at parties, "What do you do?"—the classic DC line. The classic response—"I can't exactly tell you"—has always meant, for me, "Then I can't exactly date you." But they're part of our community, the military girls, and not a few of my DC friends readily confess to a uniform fetish.

Proud to be local, to be asked directions, to know where to stand/park/maneuver at Pride events and marches, I wander about DC quite comfortably, a nice dyke in the 'hood. I was walking over to Drag King night in my tough leather jacket recently, and had to pass by a trio of blonde models having a photo session on some steps. We couldn't be more different—but *I live here.* I get to flirt with women on my block. So: "Pardon me, ladies," I said, bowing as I passed, ignoring the photographer, an older man; and the models excused me deferentially, saying to each other, "It's okay; it's just a Washingtonian passing." Interesting choice of words: genderless. But they knew they were in a gay neighborhood. My neighborhood. They named me: Washingtonian.

Big ideas, good and bad, blast through this swamp, this diplomatic wind tunnel; but don't get too attached to anything—the monuments stay up, and the restaurants close all the time. All my favorite haunts have shut their doors for good: precious, much-loved movie houses, the sauna and stage at American University, Food For Thought and Straits of Malaya, the Other Side, and Tracks. My younger lesbian herstory hides behind replastered walls, renamed edifices, reworked themes. I danced there—it's a bank now; propositioned her there—it wasn't a tapas bar back then.

In *Out of Africa*, Isak Dineson—the Baroness Karin von Blixen-Finecke—mused, "If I know a song of Africa, does Africa know a song of *me*?" Arrogant, perhaps, to write oneself into a landscape, and that author in particular was encumbered by her colonial/white intrusion onto the African continent. In the year I turned forty, I began to walk around DC feeling the weight of accumulated years, thinking, "If I know a song of Dupont Circle, does it know a song of *me*?" After all, my books are in shop windows; I'm called up to give speeches. Aware of being a think tank temp myself (that is, "permanent half-time" on the faculty of two universities) and a white Jewish woman in a black Christian city, I am also aware of my limitations in naming DC's bohemias. But much of lesbian DC has yet to be described. And I so love describing.

I want to name the daily experience of being "out" in Washington, for it's all about a love life and a political consciousness lived in the shadow of often indifferent government. Where others look at DC and see Reagan, Clinton, a couple of men named Bush, or see the shame of a football team named with a racial slur, a crime rate gone haywire, black schools in struggle while wealthy white politicians spend federal money on mistresses, I see the biggest gay bookstore in the world, the best network of women writers around, the oldest MA program in women's studies in the country, the rainbow flag on the cake. My DC isn't about affluent gay men and the Log Cabin Republicans, though they are queer Washington, too. My home is the bohemia inside the Beltway, the random photo album that spells DYKE.

And yes, every street has its girl.

Homofauxbia

Joshua Dalton

I've only been called a faggot once, at least by someone who really meant it. This asshole, Stephen, who I'd never liked, was in my high school computer class and got on my nerves. Once I wondered aloud what topic I was going to use for a project, and Stephen said from a few rows back, "He's probably gonna do gay marriage." And then, later that day, randomly, "Being gay is a choice," really loud like his volume settled the matter.

So anyway, I already didn't like him, but one day after school my friend Jessica and I were heading back to our cars when Stephen almost ran us over in, of course, a gigantic pick-up truck. I was startled and pissed and flipped him off almost automatically. He screeched to a halt, got out of his truck, stormed toward me and yelled, "Faggot! What do you think you're doing?"

I don't remember what I said back. I think Jessica tried to defend me. The ordeal left me more shocked than hurt, though, because nothing like this had ever happened before. This was Texas, yeah, but one of the nicer areas. It wasn't Arkansas. My only experiences with true homophobia had been news stories and Very Special Episodes of teen dramas, like when Marco got beat up on *Degrassi*. This persecuted feeling, it was new, and not something I wanted to feel again.

And I haven't. Not really. But lately, it's a different kind of homophobia that's gotten to me. I'm not sure what you'd call it—maybe homo*faux*bia. It's that creeping sense of discomfort when things get called "gay" or when even gay-friendly people like my college roommate, Evan, say stuff like, "I'm glad you're not flaming. Actually, you're the coolest gay guy I know. I hate those guys that are all like…."—followed by his limp-wristed, fey gay impersonation. People like Evan, I know they mean well, but it's the principle of it, you know?

A few times, I've tried to make a joke about it. "Yeah," I said to a classmate once, "this homework really *is* gay. It wants to do all the other boy homework." Most of the time, like a lot of my jokes, this goes unnoticed or misunderstood. I've had to explain with great exasperation that I was using gay in its real meaning instead of in its pejorative sense. I just wind up feeling like that moron on the playground in elementary school who, after being called a homosexual, would say, "Yeah, I *am* gay. I'm happy." Nice try, but no dice.

It's not just language. Sometimes it's the questions. I'm really looking forward to not being the Token Fag. If I have to explain "when I knew" or "am I sure" or, probably the most annoying, "catcher or pitcher?"—if I have to go through those again, I'm going to say something equally stupid back: "Catcher or pitcher? *Pfft.* I'm the umpire, man. And you don't even want to *know* what that means."

Some of these people have good intentions. Driven by curiosity, they feel like, even after barely knowing me, they can ask whatever they want. But it's not like anyone ever asks a straight guy, "So when did you realize you like pussy?"

Once I was talking to Evan about a girl he'd had over, Danica. I didn't like her because, not only did she seem stupid, she kept calling this guy that had annoyed her a faggot, making me cringe. Evan's *current* girl, Olivia, chimed in, "Well, it's not like she meant it in a bad way, though. I mean, I know a lot of people who say 'faggot,' and it doesn't have to do with being gay, it's just like, another word for a 'jerk,' or whatever."

I just nodded and said yeah. It's too uncomfortable to fight about, so most of the time I don't bother.

One time, though, I really did get upset. After Evan asked me if I thought some celebrity was hot in front of a group of guys I didn't even know, I pulled him aside later. I know he was only asking a question, and it would have been perfectly normal for him to talk about some girl being hot with the other guys. But it was like, every time someone came over, Evan just had to get my sexuality across.

"It's not like they have a problem with it or anything," he said. "I mean, they're cool."

"Yeah," I said, "but you don't have to just tell them randomly all the time. I mean, a lot of people you've told before I even met them."

And then Evan asked mc, "Do you not want them to know you're gay?" and I shut up.

Maybe I don't. Maybe I've still got "internalized homophobia" or something. Maybe I'm being hypocritical, too—I don't have nearly as strong a reaction when people throw around the N-word like it's a synonym for "guy." What does it say about me that I'm secretly offended if someone says, "Man, *Chappelle's Show*'s not on tonight, that's so gay," but I barely bat an eye when I have to hear, for the umpteenth time, some story beginning (as it seems a lot of them do), with "Man, this one nigger I know, he...."

And maybe, maybe I'm just taking things too personally. Who knows? But one thing I do know is, there's gonna be a breaking point some day. I can feel it. I mean, I can only be asked, "So, do gay guys talk all girly and stuff on purpose, or are they born doing that?" before I lash out and slap someone.

And this is coming from someone who thinks violence is, you know, totally gay.

Large and Back in Charge

Shawn Syms

The most startling thing about my years of addiction to crystal meth wasn't losing my savings, losing my friends, or losing my grip on reality—it was losing so much weight. People on methamphetamine drop pounds very quickly—and it's a crash course in how fat and thin people are treated differently.

My childhood and adolescence were typical for an outsized queer. I spent hours stretching my shirts out with my knees so they wouldn't cling to my bulging body and remind me I hated it. Despite growing up with a pool, I never learned how to swim—I was embarrassed to take my shirt off in front of other people.

Because I had a big chest to match my big belly, I was christened "Tit Man" by my sixth grade classmates. Throughout elementary school, I was mocked; in high school I was just ignored. For years, I was sad, angry, and deeply lonely. Other people marginalized because of their size have similar—and sometimes much worse—stories.

Coming of age and coming out, the emerging bear scene was a lifesaver. I'd never believed anyone would find me attractive, but was gratified to learn that some guys actually did. I even appeared once in an adult magazine for the burly, bearded set. Had I finally healed the scars of my youth and found self-acceptance? Maybe I was fine just the way I was, after all. But the lure of crystal threw all of that back into question. Some casual experimentation turned into a beguiling predicament—and fast.

Thanks to meth and late-night partying on the dance floor, I lost ten pounds in a single weekend—and then another ten pounds the following weekend. Twenty pounds in nine days. I managed to knock off another ten pounds in short order too: eating less and tweaking more. That weight loss continued, and the changes in appearance led to other shifts as well. Skinny guys are desired by many more people than fat guys. I suddenly found myself on the receiving end of more attention from other men. A *lot* more.

Perhaps I thought I'd already come to terms with my larger size before, but I was astounded and thrilled by the sudden increase in sexual privilege. Some say seeking attention based on your appearance is shallow, but I'm not ashamed to say I loved every minute of it.

I had experiences I'd never even conceived of before, like walking down the street in shorts and a tank top and having a passing group of a dozen men literally stop in their tracks to check me out. Or going to a bar where six guys rocked my world, and being approached by each and every one of them. It's almost ridiculous to recount those moments now, but at the time, my horrible world of childhood unpopularity had somehow, magically, been turned completely on its head. Frankly, those moments felt even more intoxicating for me than the profoundly addictive substance that had birthed them. Fear of regaining all that weight became a huge stumbling block to my recovery.

Not every aspect of my physical changes was positive. Though my new build appealed to many who like 'em lean and hairy, my face certainly suffered from the non-stop crystal use: persistent acne and scabs, and dark circles under my eyes that still remain. I've kept a Polaroid of myself from those days as a fateful reminder. I recall how hot I thought I was the night that photo was taken, clad only in my underwear and a seductive leer. When I look at it today, all I see are the sallow skin and hollow eyes.

Much has been made of the connection between meth and sex, but for me, that was one more area where things didn't turn out so well. Sure, I was able to have sex with greater numbers of men—and a greater variety of different types of men—because the weight loss gave me a wider range of appeal. I had a lot of sex while high, but that's partly because sex is "something to do," and when you are tweaked out and unable to sleep, you need something—anything—to do.

The sex itself was far from great. I ended up performing as a bottom almost all the time, but not because it's my natural inclination—I'm versatile but tend to prefer topping. I was stuck in a receptive role because I suffered from "crystal dick"—the inability to stay hard while tweaking.

I'm sure I was a lousy bottom anyway—my ability to give head was compromised because I was constantly dehydrated and had no saliva. And though crystal's riskiest aspect is said to be its effect on rational decision-making, I still managed to keep my wits about me and avoid contracting HIV.

One night the acute nature of my transformation came sharply into focus. It was three a.m. and I'd been dancing at The Barn, a downtown, late-night dance club. Once the bar closed, I found myself sitting on a ledge at the corner of Church and Carlton streets—restless, wide awake, and nowhere near ready to go home. A nondescript but quietly handsome guy approached me. He was clearly a working-class man, no doubt walking home from his job, maybe as a busboy, custodian, or short-order cook. He looked as if he'd probably never set foot in a gay bar; he lacked the self-conscious attention to appearance that so many gay men possess.

He looked me in the eye and said, "Would you like to come over for a while, and have something to eat?" with just a little bit of hunger in his voice. I thanked him, but said no. Food was the furthest thing from my mind. Something was wrong with this scenario, and it had nothing to do with that gentle man who was nothing but dignified. It's the fact that an adult of almost thirty should never be mistaken for a hungry street youth.

When I was finally able to force myself off the crystal train wreck, all of the weight I'd lost came piling back on. And very quickly. Crystal tricks the brain into thinking it's not hungry most of the time. With that crutch knocked out from under it, the body suddenly realizes that it has been starving for years, and tries to build up its stores of nourishment. You get up in the middle of the night and stand in front of the fridge, unable to stop eating. I gained thirty-five pounds in roughly two weeks.

Being a big man again has taken a lot of getting used to. Meth addiction shattered my body image. Since recovering, I've had many occasions where I look in the mirror and just get confused. A friend recently showed me a picture taken last Pride Day of me and another man embracing, captured from the neck down. I didn't even recognize my own body.

Now my doctor tells me that I need to lose weight because of persistent high blood pressure that puts me at risk of having a stroke. I've begun taking steps in that direction: the hour-long walk home from work, hitting the gym again for the first time in over a year, eating better, learning how to swim. I feel a need to go slowly, though, because in my life, weight loss has had complicated connotations.

I'm not sure I want to shed too many pounds; maybe just enough to get my vital signs back where they should be. I think I've finally come to appreciate being a larger-than-average man. These days, I feel a lot more secure and confident when out in public. I get fewer hassles from people—when I walk down the street, they usually step out of my way. Sex feels more natural now, and I have a lot more heft to throw behind my energetic efforts. I may not get quite as much attention as before, but that actually lends a certain tranquility that I value. Being at peace with my body seems to finally bring peace of mind.

Descend

Jason Timermanis

To be a young gay man walking into a gayborhood is to descend. My sneaker hits the queer side of the Toronto concrete and the blood ebbs from my brain, sloshing down the arteries of my neck. My center relocates itself, sinks downward. This is the true arrival, this lowering into my body.

There are signs everywhere promoting this shift. The posters glued to poles, the magazines in the stores, the men on the street, all offer up shirtless knots of muscle. The neighborhood communicates through the medium of flesh, so it's appropriate that here, at the corner of Church and Wellesley, presiding over it all, is the Botox man. He smiles serenely from his billboard on the side of the building, forehead as smooth and untroubled as a baby's ass. *Level the playing field*, he advises, and yes, he's right. Welcome to the great leveler: gay man's culture. We are all bodies here (clothing optional, of course).

More than any other social group, we gay men have used the body to understand ourselves and each other. But both flesh and ideas mature. Each generation finds itself slipping into a slightly different skin.

I

It's 1997. I'm eighteen years old in Montreal's gay village, and there's a man at the bar, much older, wrinkled, slightly stooped inside his ratty, fur-lined coat. He drinks vodka and speaks a thickly fractured English, dressed like he's headed for a rundown Eastern European social club, the kind with a MEMBERS ONLY sign in its greasy front window. He's an eccentric strain of the kind of men that populate the edges of these bars: older, solitary, and very drunk. I watch him watch me throughout the night, his eyes shining in the background like bits of wet glass. Later, when I do approach the bar, his gaze falls to the floor. *Pardon?* I say, as he mumbles something into his drink. No response.

This man doesn't want to talk. He wants only for me to ignore his drunken hand as it lurches up and tries to rest on my hip. There are dozens of these men in any gay bar on a Friday night, looking but rarely speaking. They're of a generation twice removed from mine, and speak a body language all their own. I understand enough of it to know that his hand on my hip is predation, of course, but it's also likely his most sincere attempt at communication. The urgency of his grip is saying more than his lips have ever learned to.

The bedrock of gay culture is thousands of these ordinary, awkward men who, when young, couldn't fathom being given the time and freedom to form a deep emotional connection with another man. The body was once the most they could hope for; hurried moments of release in parks and bathrooms before returning, hollow-hearted, to a wife, kids. Today's freedoms have come too late for these men whose bodies now sag and falter; they are invisible in a culture that leaves no room for elders.

The man reaches out to grasp what is most familiar—the body— and I let him. I lean over and slip my tongue into the smoky cave of his mouth. For a moment, he can have this stupid, flimsy thing: a youthful body to kiss. It's what he thinks he needs, and what, at eighteen, I'm just beginning to realize, defines me.

II

I'm nineteen, in a high-rise in Toronto, standing in the bedroom of a man a generation older than me. I've learned that my body is a key. I use it to open the doors of men's houses. A few drinks and the men take me home where I can scrutinize their lives, scan the pictures on their walls, absorb the minutiae of a stranger's life on display. I piece these men together, trying to reach some conclusion. But the objects and what they say about them differ. The only true commonality is what got me through their doors, this bodily preoccupation.

We're not alone, this man and I. In his bedroom with us is a third man, and if I have feelings for either of them, it's for the other one, likely because he's the antithesis of flesh. He has no body, is dead, a presence in the room only because of his art. It hangs on the walls, an installation piece involving plastic tigers mired in paint, their mouths full of it, sealed shut. I stare at his work as the living man sets my beer on the bedside table and takes off my shirt.

It's no surprise that the dead man died of AIDS and was carried off the way so many men were just a scant generation ahead of mine in that initial, crippling wave of the virus. My generation has inherited a legion of ghosts, but sadly they're only half formed, quickly fading. They're names on plaques in the park, an older friend's friend mentioned in passing. No one I know.

I imagine these men, dead in their prime, and the faces of the surviving men growing more pale and remote with each funeral. It's the survivors who have so firmly entrenched the body in gay culture. Confronted with the innate wrongness of young, beautiful skin harboring so much death, they refused the association, pushed back against it: a strong, beautiful body, muscled and youthful—make such a body priceless. In the face of so much young death, they glorified the flesh that still lived, flaunted it.

It's been flaunted ever since.

III

I'm twenty-seven now, older, and leading a busy life. My body is something that passes by me in mirrors as I head out the door. We're like a long-married couple, once passionate and volatile, but now settled into a peaceful, sensual cohabitation.

However reluctantly, I'm part of a lineage. Gay men were once confined to the physical. Later, corporeal devotion became protest against AIDS and its attempt to envelop gay beauty and youth. But what have I inherited now? Body worship as defiance has lost its context, spun out of control, become its own disease. My generation is a breeding ground for narcissists too often validated by the older generations with their tiresome catcalls of *work that body!*

I can't escape, not the body nor how it precedes me. I can only push against it, reject associations. Thankfully, my generation is also increasingly being defined by freedoms attained outside the bodily freeze frame of the gayborhood. We now have the choice to marry, to form same sex families, to live more visibly in straight society, but also, if we want, the choice to reject such conventionality. More than any other generation, we have the potential to find meaning outside our bodies.

When I walk into the gayborhood, the Botox ad is a sad reminder of how we limit ourselves. But when my feet are turned the other way, carrying me back out into mainstream society, the ad's pathetic sales pitch becomes a political provocation, one I can agree with. *Level the playing field,* I think as I cross the street and leave the gayborhood, choosing a life in the larger, more challenging world. I ascend.

Deep Pockets

Gayle Roberts

"Are you doing anything today?"

Those words can be the prelude to an unplanned, event-filled day of surprises, or they can mark a day of unexpected tasks. On this particular day, my friend Stewart's body language foretold the latter.

"I wasn't until now. Why?"

"I've got boxes, a fridge, a stove, and some other stuff to move from my old house. The boxes I can move in my car. With your Suburban, we could empty the house of the rest in an afternoon."

How could I say no? Stewart, a good friend for so many years, had first voiced concerns about my health six months earlier: "I'm really worried about you. Something's going on. You're stressed out. You're going to have a stroke or a heart attack."

He had been right. Something *was* wrong. I was at my breaking point, trying to cope with increasingly painful feelings of wanting to be a woman—and of hiding those feelings from friends, students, teacher colleagues, and school administrators. I was at the lowest point in my life. I knew I had to transition for peace of mind, but I was afraid. Would I, like so many of my transsexual friends, lose everything meaningful—other friends, career and, most importantly, my wife?

"It's good of you to be so concerned," I had replied. "Right now I can't tell you or anyone else what's going on with me. I'm absolutely exhausted. Maybe tomorrow night. If not, in the next few days."

I needed courage, which at that moment I did not have. Apart from my mental exhaustion, I couldn't articulate my shame about no longer having the strength to cope with my emotions. At the same time, I realized that, foolishly, I expected more of myself than I ever expected of anyone else.

My mind returned to the present. "Once the house is completely empty," Stewart was saying, "I can work on cleaning it for the new owners."

Perhaps I had been a little slow to respond to his request for help because after a short pause—as if trying to convince me to help should I be wavering—he went on, "Don't worry, you don't have to do any of the cleaning!"

"I'll be glad to help, you know that," I responded.

A lot had happened in my life since Stewart's phone call all those months ago. I finally told the school's administrators that I was a transsexual woman and that I needed time off from teaching to transition. Much to my surprise, the school board was supportive, granted me sick leave, and told me to contact them when I was ready to return. Friends supported my transition when they learned of the stress I had been under, and understood that at last I was at peace with myself. My wife also supported my transition, but grieved the loss of her husband while adjusting to our new relationship as "sisters." We agreed it was best to live apart so we could come to terms with our changed relationship. Once again, Stewart came to my aid by inviting me to stay with him.

"Do you think I'll need to wear work clothes, Stewart? Or do you think I can just wear a pair of slacks and a blouse?" It was moving day.

"You won't get that dirty, but some of the boxes we'll be moving will be covered in dust. The stove could be greasy. I'd wear work clothes."

"You know what that means?"

"No. What's the problem?"

In the weeks I'd been living with Stewart, I had bought a lot of women's clothes, for teaching and casual wear. But no women's work clothes. "I'm going to have to wear what I wore as a man," I told him.

"Is that a problem? It doesn't matter to me."

"It depends whether anybody will see me," I told him.

Before I transitioned, I tried to pass as a woman as much as I could. I wore a wig so people wouldn't see me as a man, and I wore skirts and learned how to apply makeup that gave me confidence when I was out in public. "So," I went on, "I find it ironic that, after learning to present as a woman and becoming comfortable dressed in public as one, I'm going to have to pass as a man so I can help you move! Do you know how long it took me to wash and curl my hair this morning? Well, I'll tell you. One hour! Thank God I don't have to wear that itchy wig any more. Now I'm going to have to comb my hair out so I can look more like a man."

"You're still going to help me, though?" Stewart seemed worried more about the move than about my plight.

"Of course … I'm just blowing off steam. After everything you've done for me over the years, I'm glad to help. It's just a little frustrating to have to present as a man again. I thought I'd left all that in the past. I'll need a half hour to get ready."

I found my old men's work clothes hanging in the deepest recesses of my closet, put them on, and went to the bathroom to check myself out. The curls in my hair disappeared when I stuck my head under the shower. I knew I hadn't put makeup on that morning, but I checked anyway for lipstick, mascara, and eye shadow. I wasn't afraid of presenting as a man; I was afraid of being seen as a man appearing feminine. I brushed my hair back into a male-style ponytail, then I checked in the mirror for earrings, even though I distinctly remembered taking them off the night before. Finally, confident, I left the bathroom, shouting, "I'm ready to go."

We parked the Suburban as close to Stewart's front path as possible, and he introduced me to a former neighbor, John, busy cleaning his front drive of leaves. Like me, John had a keen interest in politics, and soon we were both deep into an enthusiastic discussion. I became increasingly animated, gesticulating with my hands, focused on John, of course—until blurry red spots flashed past my face. What were they? Horrified, I focused on my hands instead of on John—and saw five bright red fingernails on each hand.

As all we women know, our clothing isn't always designed for function. Few dress slacks have pockets, and those that do have tiny slit ones able to contain little more than a pack of matches. But deep pockets are part of every man's pants, able to contain many things—tape measures, pliers, bags of nails, even hammers. And entire hands with, to my mind, out-of-character red fingernails.

Have you ever tried to resume what should be a very animated discussion with your hands buried deep in your pockets?

The Sexual Luddite

Jeffrey Rotin

I am a relic among gay men, a quaint throwback to another era.

I'm the only homo on this planet, single or attached, who doesn't cruise online. No chat rooms, no online personals, no webcam. I am the last holdout, feet firmly pressed against the portals of cyberspace, resisting its gravitational pull. I can hear the sucking sounds, like a vacuum.

If I were fending off men with a stick, it would be a non-issue. But I've been mostly unattached since a decade-long relationship ended five years ago. I'm drowning in the shallow end of the dating cesspool. "With all the options for hooking up that gay men now have at their disposal," marvels Alix, a friend of mine, "how is it possible that you're not getting laid?"

Technology has changed the landscape of dating and how we interact. Internet dating is a practical, timesaving device like a microwave or PDA: one more modern convenience. People swear by it, but I'm not convinced. Something got lost in the translation from in-person to online.

I first tested the Internet waters several years ago. A friend and I entered a chat room, curious and keen. We created accurate and—in our opinion—appealing personal profiles, but caught only a few nibbles. Underwhelmed by the response and wondering if perhaps we didn't sound so impressive on paper—he was East Indian, I was in my early forties—we crafted something more marketable, cast a wider net: "21yo college student, 6', blond, hung, straight but bi-curious." It was blatantly fake, uncreatively torn from the pages of your basic gay porn fantasy.

Within seconds, dozens of private chat invitations exploded onto our computer screen. We juggled as many conversations as we could. The questions exposed a distinct lack of imagination. "Do u have a gf?" "How big is ur cock?" "Wat do u like to do?" "Ever sucked a fat dick?"

You could practically hear the men beating off in anticipation. My friend and I laughed at the absurdity of it all, but the truth is, it gnawed at me. Being in my early forties pigeonholed me. It didn't matter that I was young at heart and didn't look anywhere near my age; if I represented myself truthfully, I was perceived as mature. A Daddy. Or more likely: out of contention. My uneasiness was compounded by bewilderment. I didn't know how to navigate hooking up on the World Wide Web, didn't understand the rules or what was expected of me. I couldn't even decipher half the messages. I had to ask what "gf" stood for.

I've checked out Internet dating sites dozens of times since then, but I still can't muster the nerve or know-how to take the plunge. I'm always overcome by a sense of foreboding that meeting guys online is a huge mistake. God knows I could easily justify my reticence. There are plenty of horror stories: the friends who are addicted and up all night cruising and chatting, the guys who post fake snapshots and lie about their age. My personal favorite: the asshole who lined up fuck dates at his loft apartment and wasn't sure whether my friend was his eight-thirty or his nine-fifteen appointment. He couldn't even remember my friend's name. Amazingly, he didn't seem to think there was anything inappropriate with his behavior. It was business as usual.

And that's the problem. Dating in the electronic age has been reduced to a business transaction. You shop from a menu of two-dimensional attributes. At the click of your mouse, a playmate can be delivered to your door in a matter of minutes. The entrails of people's most personal details are now splayed on your computer monitor in a grocery list of attributes: age, weight, height, role, sexual fetishes, dick size. And the photos—cum on a tabletop, a big black dildo shoved up an ass—titillate but obliterate any shred of imagination.

True, I've had my share of lousy encounters picking up men in bars. And time-honored cruising spots like bathhouses, parks, and tearooms aren't exactly hotbeds of intimacy and romance. They can be equally mechanical, devoid of emotion.

But what they do offer is that proximity to another body. They engage all your senses: the feel of a strong forearm, the taste of soft lips and skin, a natural body scent. The sound of a voice. A laugh. Or simply a smile. When you meet someone in person, you can't ask them to fill out a form to decide whether they meet all your criteria. You have to explore, ask questions. It's all part of the dance, the unraveling, the thrill of discovery.

For me, it's all about eye contact and that first kiss. There's an intangible chemistry, a spark, when you lock eyes. That moment of recognition when you just *know*, and the feeling is mutual. It fires up my pheromones. And a kiss, a kiss! It's a surefire way to determine if you're going to hit it off sexually, whether a roll in the hay is going to suck all the brain cells from your head and leave you wanting more.

Like the first time I met Kevin at a beer garden one Pride Day, years ago. The electricity was palpable even before we looked in one another's eyes. Standing behind me in the line-up to buy drinks, I could feel his gaze burning onto the back of my head. It was a mutual attraction. It was a *feeling*. I wanted to catch a glimpse of him but couldn't manage it without being obvious. Instead, Kevin maneuvered to step up to the bar at the same time as me. We turned to one another in quiet accord.

"Are you having a good Pride Day?" he asked. It was a disarmingly genuine opener. Staring into his steel-blue eyes, I knew right then and there I had to be with him. It was as simple as that. Never mind all the complications, that he was in the middle of a nasty breakup, that he was still living with the guy, or that I had come to the beer garden with a sort-of date. When I placed my hand under his shirt and gently touched the small of his back, felt the warmth of his skin, it was a done deal.

You can't find that kind of alchemy online. Or can you? Maybe I'm being unreasonable in my refusal to evolve with the times. Like those people who are stuck in the 1970s, with shag hairdos and acid wash jeans. Either they're boldly defiant or pathetically outcast. They fell behind and never caught up. Maybe they were afraid to change. Or maybe they were happy with the way things were and stubbornly decided to freeze-frame, style-wise. The longer they keep that seventies look, the more stuck they become.

That's me. As everyone made the leap to cyberspace, I was left floating in a stagnant puddle of obsolescence. But there's something to be said for the late seventies and early eighties dating model. Back then, you picked up a guy in a bar, went home, fucked, then got to know one another. There were no negotiations of who would do what to who, you simply figured it out as you went along. Spontaneous.

My first gay sexual experiences were like that. There was the time I was leaving a restaurant with a friend late at night. A vagrant smashed the glass panel of a bus shelter. Nearby, a cute young guy with dirty-blond hair and an athletic build was waiting for a streetcar. We exchanged glances in a *did you just see that, too?* kind of way, shrugged and smiled. Right then his streetcar arrived. Impulsively, I sprinted over, jumped on, and jostled my way through the crush of passengers to where he was standing. I told him I was heading to a party and asked him if he could tell me when we reached a particular street.

We rode in silence for a while. Then he rang the bell. "This is your stop." I stepped onto the sidewalk. He did, too.

"I lied," he confessed with a sheepish grin. "This isn't your street. This is my stop."

"I lied, too," I said. "I don't have a party to go to."

We laughed, then kissed. Back at his apartment, we shagged, chatted, smoked cigarettes, went for ice cream at four a.m. at an all-night café, and shagged some more. I remember the excitement of removing the layers of his clothes, like unwrapping a present, not knowing what to expect, and discovering to my delight that he was astonishingly beautiful and sweet and playful.

Ah, the good old days. It makes me wonder if there's a loss of innocence, or whether I've simply lost *my* innocence. I suspect it's a combination of both. It's not just the advent of AIDS; I can't shake the feeling that there's something cutthroat about online cruising. Now, everything seems super-sized and dressed to impress. Maybe I'm mildly delusional to think that chasing after a complete stranger in a streetcar was more, well, romantic. Maybe I'm just not up for the competition these days. Somehow it seems more brutal to be rejected after providing someone with all your stats—though I wouldn't know because I still haven't had the balls to try and pick up someone online.

During agonizingly slow periods I still grapple with the dilemma of whether to go with the flow and join the online revolution. But I can't, it's just not in me. Call me old-fashioned, call me crazy, but I'll stick to my guns and hold out for that eye contact, that touch, that first magical kiss.

Words

Therese Szymanski

Geek, butch, girlfriend, nerd, lesbian. Such words—such labels—used to be constricting, now they're liberating. For instance, when I graduated from high school, none of them described *me*.

In 1997, when I walked into my ten-year high school reunion, most of those words still didn't apply to me. *Queer, gay,* and *lesbian* all belonged to me, however, and felt right on my shoulders.

And as I looked around the room, I said to my "date," "Outta here right after dinner?"

Kevin nervously glanced about. "Yeah, I think so." Neither of us fit during high school, and we didn't expect that to change.

Earlier that year, while she was in town visiting me, my girlfriend wanted to meet up with an online friend at a local lesbian bar. There, a big, bearded blond guy came up to me and said, "Therese? Therese Szymanski? It's me, Kevin. Kevin Score, from McDonald's."

Score. Oh. *Kevin.* No *Score.* He had worked with me at McDonald's and ended up dating Donna. He had spent all his money on her, and she got pregnant by her *ex*-boyfriend.

It suddenly all made sense. His words back then hadn't been nice, and I'd participated in some of them, and only now, as I write this, do I realize all the ironies of it, because each day opens more power to the words.

But that night, my girl and her friend chatted while Kevin and I caught up, eventually remembering we'd been in the same high school graduating class. During high school I worked full-time as a McDonald's manager, so, really, it wasn't odd that we forgot we went to school together. After all, we never saw each other there, because he was in general curriculum courses while I took college prep, but he was on my work shifts about sixteen hours a week.

Back in high school, all of the 424 students knew who I was, and it seemed that they all had opinions of me as a stick-up-the-butt brainiac, McDonald's manager, non-partier, or class brain.

Meanwhile, as the closing Mickey D's swing manager on the weekends, I'd formed the After Close Drinking Crew. The security guard was our designated buyer, and his little brother was in my year, but not in any of my classes. The guard would sometimes keep our leftover booze at his parents' house, where he lived, and his younger brother remarked, years later, that he had walked into a class one day while a bunch of classmates were talking about how I never drank or did anything wrong. He sat down remembering the half-fifth of Don Q 151 rum sitting at his house that belonged to me.

He knew I could out-drink most of the football team, so he had his own inside laugh that day in class.

When I was a freshman in college, my folks went on a trip during spring break. One night when I wasn't working, I threw a party at their house. When someone on my dorm floor found out about it, she invited a neighbor of my old security guard. This neighbor, who also went to my college and had been in my graduating class, couldn't believe Miss Stick-in-the-Mud was capable of partying, let alone throwing a party.

They had a lot of words for me back then, during high school and college: *geek*, *nerd*, *goody-two-shoes*, *brain*. Same meanings, different words, and none of them felt comfortable, felt like *me*.

But then, after high school, I started finding words that fit, like *dyke*. And then, sometime after the reunion, I'd own *butch*, reown *nerd* and *geek* and, finally, realize I could be the *girlfriend* and not just have a girlfriend.

My high school was in a city just north of Detroit, a blue-collar town that was, at the time, considered the whitest large city in the country. Students at that school did not know very many words, especially words that might help them think about people and diversity.

The guy who changed watch batteries at a booth in the mall had been in my class as well. One day, he suggested that if we were having a reunion, the easiest way to find old classmates would be to canvass Jackson State Penitentiary.

My girlfriend dumped me. I found a new girlfriend. I bought two tickets to the reunion. Then the new girlfriend dumped me too.

Kevin and I had kept in touch, so when he got dumped as well, he just picked up my spare and we went together.

His greatest joy upon our arrival at the reunion was noticing how many of our former classmates were now bald, but not even that alleviated our feelings of awkwardness. Sure we recognized people, but I'm terminally shy and he seemed to be following my lead. We agreed to make a hasty retreat as soon as we were done eating so we'd have plenty of time to hit our respective Blockbusters and spend some quality movie time by ourselves.

That didn't happen.

I'd never heard any slurs about my sexuality at my high school. Never been called *dyke* or *queer.* In fact, I only heard about it for the first time when I was in my mid-thirties and caught up with an old McDonald's crewmember, who admitted that after I left people frequently asked my best friend, another crewmember-turned-manager, about me, always with insinuations like, "Oh, so you're going up to Michigan State *to spend the weekend with her.*"

I hate that she had to deal with the allegations, especially since neither of us ever had any of the fun that should have come with them.

When I signed up for the reunion, I was supposed to write a short bio detailing what I'd been up to since high school. I wrote about my job, degree, produced plays and published books, any of which might have been enough to get folks talking to us after the meal—let alone the wives asking husbands who the woman in the suit was—but none of those got as many people talking to us as did the last two words of my bio: *Happily Queer.*

I'd been different in high school, and people usually weren't too surprised when I did something unexpected, like having the Math Club pose for our yearbook photo while hanging upside down on the baseball fence. So that night at the reunion, my bio gave everyone an opening to come up and say they'd always expected something different from me. They were of course commenting on the books and such, but they all also mentioned the queerness—especially one woman who said, "I've been coming out to everyone I can tonight, so you won't be the only one!"

People I'd been friends with in elementary school chatted with me, including the two girls (who went on to become cheerleaders) who used to tie me up. Alas, not in a fun way: they had helped me practice my magic tricks, including the fabulous chain-and-rope escape.

Kevin and I became a focal point of the party, and he was surprised by all the people I'd known. For instance, Steve, one of the co-captains of the football team, remarked that he couldn't believe I'd come out in the program—this was Warren, Michigan, for God's sake! He then congratulated me and bought me a drink. Danny had also been a friend in elementary school, but he grew up to be a small-town, rednecky sheriff—and he dressed the part, wearing more incorrectly sized polyester than an entire small town should be allowed to wear. The years hadn't been friendly to him.

Accepting words has made me grow. Years ago, I'd only viewed *butch* by stereotypically defined definitions, thoughts that were fertilized and grew rampant with help from girlfriends of the times. I grew to accept the word and take it over, and whole new worlds of belonging opened up for me. I became more myself when I stopped running from the words and accepted them, and myself.

My mother had a plaque hanging in the house I grew up in: *It's what you learn after you know it all that counts.*

I knew a lot of words back then. I know more now.

I got an email the other day from Steve. He wants me involved right from the get-go in planning the twenty-year reunion. My new girlfriend says she never, ever expected me to be the sort to have anything at all to do with a high school reunion.

Geek, butch, girlfriend, nerd, lesbian ... me.

Altered People

Gregory Woods

> And up the paths
> The endless altered people came,
> Washing at their identity.
> —Philip Larkin, "An Arundel Tomb"

1

On October 14, 2003, I ejaculated semen for the last time. The next morning I went into hospital for a trans-urethral resection of the prostate. Although a minor operation for men by comparison with a hysterectomy, it still carries some of the latter's symbolic weight. The manopause is a lesser sibling to the menopause. Signaling the end of reproductive capability, it is effectively the closure of the period of active sexuality that began with puberty. In many patients, myself included, one of its side effects is impotence. You might say it marks the beginning of old age.

2

Yet I was only fifty at the time. For most men this operation is not needed for at least another decade. That momentous last ejaculation was self-induced, a last-minute hand-job before I went to sleep the night before the op. (The great god Pan is dead!) Not that sex is at an end for me, but the climax without outcome is like a boy's. I miss the pleasure of the actual flood of the semen down the length of the urethra. Still, what is lost in intensity of orgasm is gained in not having to boil-wash the sheets so often.

3

I regret my new condition or status. But I do not regret regret. As poets have always known, it offers its own pleasures. Regret is one of my familiars, like a witch's scrawny, yowling cat. From the start, it was built into my sense of myself as a gay youth—mainly because I so often thought of things I might have said to boys I fancied long after I had failed to say them. Even allowing for the adjustments of growing confidence and quicker-wittedness, this has since become a lifelong habit, unwilled and unwanted—regretted, indeed. Contrary to much of what our televisions and the advertising industry try to tell us, happiness is not the only satisfying emotional state. We never seem to be allowed to celebrate and luxuriate in our sadnesses—not even after everything we learned about ourselves in the worst extremes of the AIDS epidemic.

4

Post-manopausal, have I become someone else? Having labored so long, so long ago, to come out and stay out of the closet, must I now go in again? Has my queer membership lapsed? Should I hand in my insignia? Since the 1960s, gayness has been configured in the West as an identity that is predominantly male, white, young, urban and, above all, sexually involved. It has always been more difficult to be gay if one does not personally conform to any of these characteristics. But the last of them was the most important. It was the proof—as a Roman Catholic would say in another context—the outward sign of inward grace.

5

By the standard of such involvement, I was always a queer type of queer. When I had sex I did not talk about it. When I had love I did not take a vow of fidelity and perpetuity. I have never lived as half of a couple. I have never had what you could call a boyfriend. Although

I am a professor of gay and lesbian studies and should keep myself informed about such things, I simply cannot be bothered to read the debates about gay marriage and gay parenting. I am not interested. People are individuals. I sicken at the thought that someone else might become so close to me that he would presume to finish my sentences on my behalf. Even relying on other people for sexual pleasure strikes me, at times, as redundant and inefficient.

6

I want to do to another person—whether he be a boy in the flesh, in pornographic representation, or in pure fantasy—all those things that feminists object to in male heterosexual desire: to objectify him, to fetishize him, to exploit him (whether actively or passively). For me, the erotic is implacable and uncompromising. This is not to say that I have never loved, and loved deeply, with that insanity that takes over every aspect of one's life until agony and ecstasy seem indistinguishable and inseparable.

7

I have traveled as far in masturbatory fantasy as in my reading life. In his book *Homos*, Leo Bersani asked an important question that has not been given much thought since adolescent self-abuse ceased to be regarded as a definitive symptom of degeneracy: "Who are you when you masturbate?" When you go back to a supposedly adolescent sex-style of solitary (but always peopled) onanism, who do you become?

8

We know that the major part of sex takes place in the brain. Dare I say, then, that the location of my queerness has always been cerebral rather than genital? Identity is not a matter of the body, even if parts of the body may be marked (or identified) by it—in circumcision, for instance, or tribal tattooing. We often recognize each other by aspects of physical appearance, but that is no more who we are than our smell or the sounds of our voices.

9

My prostate operation, that trans-urethral resection, was carried out (under a general anaesthetic) by the insertion of the cutting instrument up the length of my penis. It had the side effect of broadening my urethra, and therefore the flow of my piss, and changing the shape and feeling of my erection (if any). Far more invasive than my first experience of being anally fucked, more than thirty years previously, this procedure could, if I allowed it to, define me for the remainder of my life, like some kind of reverse puberty. There is something attractive about this idea, even if I think of myself as having been mutilated. Having been altered, I want to be that altered person. As Parolles says in *All's Well That Ends Well*, after he has been humiliated and disgraced, "simply the thing I am / Shall make me live."

10

After the operation, you piss blood for weeks. When I thought this had been going on for too long, I decided to phone my uncle, who, although thirty years older than me, had recently had the same op himself. He is an ex-army officer, erstwhile arms dealer to one of the Gulf States, very right wing, with a clipped, barking voice, toothbrush mustache, and rigidly upright bearing. I do not remember ever having had an intimate conversation with him. But now we swapped gory personal details as if to the manner born. We were altered, two incompatible characters suddenly bonding over what he called "the old waterworks."

11

I do not think of my happy new state of existence as celibacy, since that term denotes a moral choice and I neither think of sex as sinful nor of myself as a sinner. No, the condition to which I have ascended in my balmy mid-fifties is my second not-coming: a second virginity, virginity squared, virginity queered. Quentin Crisp was not being frivolous when he named one of his books *How to Become a Virgin*. I am a suburban, middle-aged neo-virgin, luxuriating in regret. How queer is that?

12

There is more to life than sex, and more to life even than one-to-one love. As W.H. Auden wrote in "First Things First," "Thousands have lived without love, not one without water." It is possible to survive without couple-dependency—Plato's supposed twinning of souls—and without that squirt of slime we figure as ecstasy. What else is there, you ask? Shooting at cats, if you are William Burroughs. Otherwise? Reading good books, for a start; then eating and laughing with friends.

Daughters of Zelophehad

Karen Taylor

Between my first lesbian crush and my first lesbian lover, I started converting to Judaism. The decisions leading up to my conversion were a combination of logic and faith, with a touch of mystery. How appropriate, then, that these passions be reflected in my sexual journey, too. But which of the Biblical journey stories do I use as a metaphor?

The "Lekh Lekha" story of Abraham is also about initiation, a tale of risking unknown territory, moving only on faith. There is Jacob's erotic wrestling with an angel, complete with a sexually rough twist of the thigh. There is Joseph, the pretty boy, a dreamer dressed in a robe of rainbows, who spurns the attentions of women and cries when he is given the chance to return to the arms of his family.

But mine is a quintessentially female journey, and as such, is filled with women. My journey includes that moment, standing in the middle of the desert halfway between Moab and Bethlehem, telling myself and the woman I am with, "Wherever you go, I will go, your God will be my God." It is the story of my love for women. And it is why my Hebrew name is Ruth—named for a woman who sees the strength Judaism gave another woman, and became the first convert and great-grandmother of King David.

My journey begins in Seattle at the height of the "Harmonic Convergence" frenzy. I went to queer-run "EST-esque" weekends filled with hungry seekers agonizing in their coming-out process and looking for a quick fix of revelation. As with the wrestling between Jacob and his angel, the language for sexuality and spirituality became co-mingled. But the encounters between the participants felt too shallow; the weekend left me terribly aware of the God-shaped hole in my soul that could not be filled with incense and angel cards. I sought a more primitive, visceral experience. I wanted a tangible religion with ritual and blood and tears and sweat and a sense of purpose.

Was it only coincidence that I also sought the same visceral emotions in my sexual encounters?

The first woman I had a crush on was a Jewish lesbian. She was round, warm, and happily and actively sexual. She taught me to flirt, and threw herself passionately into arguments with me on topics ranging through sex, feminism, politics, and religion as if arguing such important things were part of being a lesbian, part of being a Jew. Once, she kissed me, and I tingled when I felt her breasts crushed into my own. She and I explored sadomasochism, finding our paths and showing off our bruises and bite marks over coffee in the morning.

My first female lover was a Jewish woman. She was butch, but not in a swaggering macho way—she could pass as a yeshiva boy, pale and intense. Small, almost fragile, she exuded a powerful sense of herself. She had not been to a synagogue in years, but kept the laws of kashrut, and taught me my first prayers in Hebrew. She cooked, she read, she ironed her dress shirts and polished her boots meticulously, and admired femme women enormously. She was also the first person ever—including myself—to bring me to multiple orgasms. She taught me to ask for what I wanted in bed, then encouraged me to expect it from her and future lovers. She taught me to get her off with fingers, tongue, lips, sex toys, and my voice. She showed me how to masturbate in different positions, and fisted me during my menstrual cramps to provide an internal massage—and to demonstrate that a sexual act without orgasm was also an acceptable, intimate act. She never separated sexuality from the rest of her life; it was as integral to her as her Judaism.

This was how I wanted to be. Not just sexually, although certainly that way, too. This was how I wanted to move through the world.

Was it the lesbianism or the Judaism that enabled these women to be like this? As the rabbis would say, yes and yes.

And so like Abraham, I left my home and began my journey. When I began my conversion at a local synagogue, I spent time with the synagogue's librarian, a bisexual woman. She introduced me to essays of Jewish women confronting and challenging their beliefs and their sexuality. She invited me to my first seder. Yes, I would think as I studied, this is where I want to be. I want to struggle with myself and with other women, body and soul. I want to fully engage myself, challenge assumptions, question beliefs. I want to immerse myself in the mikvah, fast for Tisha Ba'av, eat in a fragile sukkah with the wind blowing through my hair. I want to feel my religion as physically as I feel an orgasm.

More and more, my life filled with Jewish women. In fact, it filled with Jewish lesbians, the true descendants of the daughters of Zelophehad. Who? These displaced women have a brief, but important moment in Exodus. The daughters of Zelophehad learn that Moses is going to announce that only men can inherit property in the Promised Land, and demand a hearing. The daughters—recently orphaned and without brothers or husbands—collectively and passionately demand a right to the inheritance of Israel. God sides with the women, asserting that they do indeed have the right to be part of Jewish history and tradition. Their story is briefly told, but its impact on me was transformative: God says we do have a place in the world, we women without men in our lives.

My daughters of Zelophehad were the first women I ever met who talked about sex as a joyful, erotic, and passionate act. These women loved the variety of shapes and sizes of women's bodies and minds. They loved women as friends, as sexual partners, and as objects of lust. They talked frankly about ways they had sex with each other or by themselves, and how it evolves over time with different partners and as we age. They talked about the passion of power and ritual manifested sexually and religiously. They talked about orgasms as if they were a part of life to which all women were entitled, as much a part of life as eating and breathing. All this easy sexuality between women upset the natural order of heterosexuality, of course. But these were the daughters of Zelophehad: they knew that God had given them this place, and embraced them fully. So when it became my time to stand in the desert, halfway between choices, I, like Ruth, chose to travel to my new life in the company of God and the company of women.

The final step in converting to Judaism is to meet before a trio of rabbis, a bet din, and to immerse three times in a ritual bath, a mikvah. When I met with the rabbis, one of them asked me, "Do you understand that by taking on this faith, you may be the object of stereotypes and hate crimes?" I chuckled, and said "Rabbi, I'm a lesbian." He paused, then joined my laughter, saying, "So, you're coming out as a Jew!" After a moment, the other two rabbis joined us, laughing at this simple but real expression of truth. I was to be a Jew, a daughter of Zelophehad. I would have a place in the world.

My life journey has taken me across the country to New York, the great city of the Jewish diaspora. I am surrounded by Jews of all ages, backgrounds, and passions. I am home in a way inexpressible by anyone but Ruth, who is welcomed "back" to Bethlehem, a city she has never been to before, but one she travels to with Naomi, completing her journey. I am immersed, as I was in the mikvah, by a vibrant, passionate place that expects me to make my way through it, through tears and laughter, wrestling and dancing.

My spouse, my helpmeet, is another Jewish lesbian convert. We started our journeys separately, and built a Jewish home together.

We married under a chuppah, wrapped together in a tallis, standing before our families and our community, drinking the heady taste of wine after a day of fasting in preparation for the ceremony. We were lifted on chairs and danced ourselves into exhaustion. I look into my partner's eyes, knowing that God created us, all of us, in God's image. I remember these things as I lean over my lover's body to kiss her in that sensitive area on her thigh, the place touched by an angel, the place that makes us weak from wrestling and names us Israel: "God-wrestlers." I bless God for making me part of the heritage of rebel women, daughters of Zelophehad, the troublesome, passionate, and necessary women of our world. I am proud to be among them.

Hecklers and Christians

David Hatfield Sparks

Stealing a kiss from you in public, I stiffen slightly and check the four directions for hecklers and Christians. For at this crossroads, saviors come pandering guilt and hate in pamphlet form.

I wait for our daughter to call. She has not contacted us in two years because we, her radical gay fathers, have, we speculate, reminded her too often and too bluntly that she was raised, even in these anti-feminist times, to be fiercely independent, not to ignore herself and her career, not to focus the bulk of her energy on being a devoted wife and mother—a mother to children we are to have nothing to do with.

San Francisco Mission District, 1993: I stand, empty-armed, stunned. While caring for my daughter's partner's infant nephew, I suddenly hear the slamming of doors and the heavy stomp of feet up the stairs, only to see the infant's father glaring at me. He is looking at me with horror, with a look that could kill. A newly converted Jehovah's Witness, full of homophobic hate, he grabs the infant from me and rushes downstairs.

In the past, when our reluctant in-laws were primarily Catholic, we were simply avoided, not spoken to, our presence invisible at parties and family gatherings. Now, it seems, we, despite our former role as the "good parents," have become devilish, imagined moral and physical threats to the children. We will not be permitted a part in this extended straight family—a family that is now able to accept my daughter and her partner's relationship due to the illusion of heterosexuality in their union, because their "blood" family member, having discovered her/his transgender nature, has transitioned from female to male—a transition we, his queer family, not his blood family, supported.

They now are married, appearing in familial and public eyes a "normal" couple, while my partner and I remain visibly gay men, and as such are vilified and exiled by "in-laws." Sadly, my daughter and her partner seem to have acquiesced to the family's view, as they have ceased to include us in the warp and woof of their lives, instead choosing to devote their energies to that extended and multi-ethnic family.

My partner and I have been deeply scarred by these unimagined events. There now appears fresh stigmata on queer hearts, new injuries for queer warriors already scarred by the existential battles we wage daily.

We have walked hand-in-hand, climbed San Francisco streets, strolling down the campus's main drag in Austin, Texas, been chased by teenage thugs with knives or by red-necked ramblers with whiskey breath; we have been surrounded by bellowing street preachers and queer-baiting hecklers, biblical "proofs" and militant hymns shaking like death's rattle over our sodomite heads, decked out in head scarves, earrings, and political buttons; we have passed a father who covers his young son's eyes, advising him, "Don't look at that, don't look at them kind!

But when I recall the innocence and tenderness of lovers, or the bliss of holding my newborn daughter, I try to enshrine those memories like talismans of joy and promise. Yet contradictions and ironies swirl around me like tempests. Having come through so much—divorce, coming out, a custody battle—how have I ended up at this juncture?

> Whenever I crossed the Missouri River coming into
> Nebraska the very smell of the soil tore me to pieces.
> I could not decide which was the real and which the
> fake "me".… I knew every farm, every tree, every
> field in the region around my home, and they all
> called out to me.
> —Willa Cather

Many gay men from rural backgrounds like myself reflect on an adulthood of urban exile and a rural childhood of nature, family, and church. I am haunted by memories of endless cornfields, perfume of newly mown alfalfa, mysteries of ancient barns and ice cream socials, and of green felt boards pinned with Holy Land maps in summer Bible School. While my immediate family lost their land and moved into town, my close relatives remained on farms. The distance between town and their farms is less than a ten-minute walk through the 4H County Fairgrounds, where during harvest or fair season I might help out.

My parents were not churchgoers, nor was my suffragette, librarian grandmother. I probably attended church more often than the three of them, immersing myself in the meager rituals and rousing hymns of rural America. When alone in church practicing on the organ, I felt certain of some deity's presence. Yet when I was baptized in a creek at a summer church camp, I was let down, not experiencing the holy insight the minister had promised. I began to wonder what kind of person Jesus was calling me to be, what kind of home He was calling me to create.

I have two photos that provide moments of clarity, memories that shake me out of childhood reverie. No more than six years old, I am seated in front of my phonograph in a long calico skirt and moccasins listening to records. I am about twelve years old, posing with cousins near the fireplace at my grandmother's. In the first photo

I remember being concerned that my dog sit still beside me. In the second, I have the look in my eye of someone who's just realized that he does not belong, not to the relatives standing beside him, not to the church, not to Jesus, not to any part of the close-knit community he knows like the back of his hand, of someone who has realized that he will one day feel forced to abandon his hearth and home—its dogwood trees, suppers of freshly picked tomatoes, its hallowed tombstones—for some gayer urban mecca.

San Francisco, 1981: We have made the trek from the Mission to Civic Center. The city's streets are a maze of maskers promenading in Gay Pride. We're dressed as genies, while our daughter, a whirlwind of spangles and scarves, is fascinated with drag queens. We march alongside a few other queer families. As we wind down Market Street, a covey of Radical Faeries hisses at us: "Breeders!" Only a short time ago, gay men with babies were not all the rage. When my daughter and I shopped in the Castro ghetto, we encountered disapproving stares. When we ate burgers at gay dives or attended classic camp movies, we were treated to disparaging remarks about children. Potential lovers were turned off when I introduced my daughter.

For several years in the early 1980s, my partner and I were involved in a custody battle for my daughter. This was due, in part, to her stepfather's alleged abuse, her mother's institutionalization during a bout with mental illness, and our belief that she would grow stronger and flourish with us. The progressive organizations we thought might offer assistance refused. Queers and women we encountered told us that a child, especially a daughter, no matter the environment, belonged with her mother. Our fight against "a woman" was judged as misogynist. Were we pederasts? Other radical men's groups and leaders, disapproving of bisexuality and previously married queers, officially excluded children, and us, from their gatherings, communities, and publications. Arguments and excommunicates ensued, lines were drawn, and opposing camps formed.

One friend, Gloria Anzaldúa, a radical Chicana lesbian writer, and one organization, the Sisters of Perpetual Indulgence, an order of drag nuns, fought for us to have the right to raise our daughter. Being jeered at as "breeders" and blackballed from A-list queer groups constitutes what I now think of as a form of queer fundamentalism, one clothed in carnival garb, but just as zealous as any Baptist rant. We have all felt the judgment of our own communities for not being "enough," of not conforming to some popular variety of radical belief or chic behavior. I often think of Audre Lorde's line, "I do not believe that all our wants have made our lies holy."

I'm waiting for my daughter to call. These days when I speak to close women friends, feminists, and others, it's different. They commiserate with me about prodigal daughters. Queers with babies are the new radical chic. Committed couples are "married," not told they are "anti-progressive" or "hetero-imitative." But some things haven't changed. Anita Bryant has been displaced by the Rick Santorums, by the Bush dynasty, by too many Democratic party pundits decrying the evils of gay marriage and queer parenting. Contradictions and ironies that once washed over me now threaten to freeze me. I feel like I'm again playing that childhood game Statues. But now I'm a blindfolded adult, flung far afield by hostile forces, to unpredictably "freeze" into an unflattering form, into an asinine sculpture. Still, I remain vigilant when we kiss in public. Now I check the four directions, plus my own kith and kin, for hecklers and Christians.

Conduct Unbecoming

Stan Persky

When I arrived at US Naval Air Detachment vr-24, based at the Capodichino military airport a few kilometers outside the port of Naples, Italy, I almost immediately met my invisible double.

At the barracks, located a short way from the hangars, someone showed me to the bunk I'd been assigned, a rack of criss-crossed strips of metal and a rolled-up mattress, the place where I'd sleep for the next two years. There were four bunk beds to a "cubicle" that was partitioned from other identical cubicles by a wall of metal lockers in which to stow our gear. One of my cubicle mates, a shrewd wiry kid from Arkansas named Birdsall, mentioned that the bunk and locker I was about to occupy had belonged to Charlie S., whose replacement I was.

When I reported in at the hangar to Petty Officer First Class Parr—I'd been assigned to work as a clerk in the detachment's administration office, which was located upstairs at the back of the hangar—it turned out that I had been given Charlie S.'s old job as well as his desk. From the office windows, one looked down onto the oil-stained hangar floor, where the small t-37s and medium-sized cargo-carrying dc-3s were wheeled in and maintained by the company's electricians and mechanics, who were, among the enlisted ranks, the "real men" of the outfit, compared to us "pencil pushers."

Parr was a gruff, not especially friendly man, a career sailor who had somehow not risen to the rank of chief petty officer, which he ought to have attained, given the number of "hashmarks" on the forearm of his uniform, signifying years of service. Perhaps that soured him somewhat. It may have been from him that I learned that Charlie S. came from Chicago, as did I.

But it was Birdsall who told me the story. Though unschooled, he was worldly-wise, possessing a kind of commonsense sophistication that I frequently encountered among boys raised in farming communities in the American South. He told me that Charlie—who was now in a navy brig in Norfolk, Virginia—was in the process of being dishonorably discharged for homosexuality. Charlie, Birdsall insisted, wasn't a fruit. He wasn't even necessarily a homo; he was just a friendly, joke-telling, regular guy who simply liked sex a lot. It was clear that Birdsall had been friends with Charlie, as had many others in the company.

What had happened was that one night Charlie, along with a couple of other guys from the outfit, had gone out to an abandoned plane parked in a nearby field behind the barracks, ostensibly to drink a few beer. The little party, enlivened by the entertaining, joke-telling Charlie, became ever pleasanter, looser. Talk turned, as it often did, to how horny everyone was. In any case, one thing led to another and Charlie sucked off the two other guys. Birdsall figured that it was mostly a matter of high spirits rather than exclusive sexual preference, since Charlie often went with the guys into Naples for a night of drinking and sex with the women from the local bar (a sailor's hangout that I would in due course also come to know).

"Shee-it," snorted Birdsall. "If he'd asked me, I'd probably have gone out to the plane with him, too." Since Birdsall was telling this story in the presence of several of our cubicle mates, all listening attentively and none objecting to his account, it was clear that the lack of disapproval was a generally shared opinion.

Word had gotten around. Charlie and the guys he'd blown were called in for questioning by the company officer responsible for such matters. They got scared and blabbed. Now all three of them were being kicked out, since the navy regulation prohibiting homosexuality underscored the fact that no distinction was made between "active" and "passive" participants. The official phrase was "conduct unbecoming" a member of the US Armed Forces. Birdsall saw it as just bad luck that they had been caught. All of this had happened only a month or so before I arrived.

There was a recent letter from Charlie to Birdsall, written from the Norfolk brig. Birdsall handed it to me, and I can still see the lined paper, the blue ink, and Charlie's looping handwriting, which I occasionally ran across in the files at the detachment office. The letter was a chatty account of life in the brig, which wasn't at all pleasant for prisoners about to be discharged for homosexual acts. But his account showed that Charlie was taking it in stride, irrespective of the public humiliation to which he had been subjected (humiliation whose magnitude, at this late date, is barely describable or imaginable). It was a friendly letter, unapologetic, and it struck me as the kind of thing one might write from summer camp to one's pals back home.

How extraordinary this all was. I'd been assigned more or less randomly to a place in the world in which I was figuratively stepping into the shoes and literally occupying the bunk and doing the job of a boy from the same city and with the same desires as me. The odds against such a coincidence must have been enormous. If Birdsall would have gone off to the abandoned airplane and let himself be blown there by Charlie, I would just as surely have been willing to go there too and perform the very act on Birdsall (who was certainly attractive to me) that Charlie was no longer available to do. How strange and oddly thrilling to come so far only to encounter a mirror image of oneself, a genuine *Doppelgänger*.

In the event, I never went out to the plane or blew Birdsall. But I was passionately, crazily in love the entire time I was there, infatuated with one agemate after another, with several at once, with groups of them. I was also sufficiently terrified by the evident consequences of acting on my desire to—as they say in the military—proceed with utmost caution. There are dozens of tales in this sea-locker—of sailors, longing, sex, friendships, landscapes, art, Naples itself, flights in airplanes, leaves to Paris—the dowry of a future storyteller. But in the autobiography of how I came to bear a blue tattoo of a ship's anchor on my forearm, there are only two I absolutely need.

I fell in love for what seemed like a surprisingly long time, a year or more, with one of the guys in the barracks, a dark-haired, lean-limbed boy I'll call Bob Cassidy. At the same time, I became best friends with David Martin, a sturdy, sensible, old-family Californian with whom I shared intellectual and artistic interests. We often went drinking together, took trips to nearby sights, read the same books.

Cassidy may have been a Californian too. If he was, he was probably a transplanted one, raised in some fringe eastern urban center and then, probably through parental break-up, shifted to an equally seedy southern California version. The other guys didn't much like him; they considered Cassidy fundamentally untrustworthy, a bit rat-like with his sly grin. And indeed, when he crawled out of the sea onto the sand, his black hair slicked back, there was something slightly feral about his dark, glistening eyes. I took a set of photographs of Cassidy in which he was wearing black-and-white vertically striped bathing briefs, exuding precisely the combination of sexy charm and deceit that made others distrust him and me love him. The photos were taken on Ischia, an island in the Bay of Naples, where we spent a weekend together some time after the incident I'm thinking of now.

I'd rented a room in a villa-like building quite close to the base, another place to sleep, where I could spend time by myself, have friends over, make a routine slightly different from the barracks' enforced collectivity. One night I invited Cassidy over. I don't remember the details, or what phase of the relationship we'd reached, except that I was in pretty deep. In fact, I've clearer memories of confiding my yearnings for Cassidy to my all-purpose artistic and romantic adviser, David, than of being with Cassidy himself. Except for this incident.

We spent the evening talking and drinking. It got late. I suggested to Cassidy that he could sleep over. That was okay by him. I didn't have a plan, maybe not even an intention, simply a mixture of self-deceptively high-minded ideas about love and about lust rubbed raw.

He snoozed. He was wearing jockey-type white underwear that I could see in the dark along with the slight bulge at the crotch. Gathering up my courage or perhaps simply driven by desire, I reached across an infinite gap. I tried to persuade myself that my touching him was tentative enough that I still had an avenue of retreat if he "woke" and objected.

I crawled between his legs as I fondled his growing, hardening cock. He lifted his small butt an inch and in a swift single movement slid off his underpants. Cassidy knew exactly what was going on all along and had no objections. My mouth closed over his erection.

I was surprised by the generous thickness of a sexual organ I had failed to imagine adequately, a size that seemed much larger against the general leanness of his body. Inexperienced as I was, the actual dimensions of reality bumped up against the image of a dream boy whom I'd totally etherealized.

As I strained forward to get more of him into my mouth, lying between Cassidy's spread legs, my belly pressed into the bed, the slight friction of my body against the sheets was enough to release all those months of pent-up passion. After I came, I stopped blowing him. He turned on the bedside lamp. Still half-mesmerized by the sight of his fully erect cock, but already feeling the discomfort of the night air cooling the sticky goo in my crotch, I asked, "Do you want me to go on?" Cassidy utterly kept his aplomb. "It's up to you," he said. Instead, we talked. He slipped his underpants back on. I used a towel to dry off.

In retrospect, it was an idiotic beginner's mistake not to finish him off. It would have given me some much-needed experience, him some pleasure, and would have cost neither of us anything, as well as creating future prospects for the repetition of the experience. What others saw as Cassidy's untrustworthiness was exactly what I trusted to keep his mouth shut and us out of trouble. In the ensuing talk, he asked one slightly grammatically and semantically tangled question that I see as the point of this story.

"Is it me or is this a ... a problem for you?" Cassidy asked. I immediately understood him; skip the sociological word "problem." I could tell from his tiny stutter that he just couldn't think of another way to put it at the moment. What Cassidy was asking was, *Has this happened because you're in love with me specifically, or are you a homosexual?* Intentionally or not, it also offered me an easy way out. I took it. "It's you," I said truthfully enough. But the point was—and this is what it would still take me a while to sort out—both halves of the equation were equally true. I would love specific others *and* the desire was homo.

There's not much more. I reported in excitedly to my confidant, David, who seemed suitably impressed by my daring. I described it all in the third person, as if we were characters in the story I'd been trying to write about Cassidy and myself. And just now I'm suddenly remembering—that is, I can "hear"—David's throaty chuckle, a unique sound never heard before or since.

Despite my attempts at art, I remained as stupid as ever in interpersonal affairs. Cassidy and I spent a weekend together on the island of Ischia some weeks after that incident. We slept in the same room, there was all that changing into and out of vertically striped black-

and-white bathing suits, showers, generous views of butts and balls; it never occurred to me that Cassidy was offering me a chance at a repeat performance.

It was about a year later. I remember the time fairly precisely because on August 13, 1961 (a day that falls within this period), the East German government began building the Berlin Wall, and there was a good chance that my tour of duty, which was almost over, would be extended "for the duration," as they say in military-speak. The "crisis" passed and I was discharged as scheduled.

If I were writing fiction, I'd probably turn Cassidy and a boy named Jimmy Joe K. into a single composite. But I'm not, and I won't. I was certainly as much, or as desperately, depending on how you look at it, in love with Jimmy Joe K., a blond-haired apprentice airplane mechanic, as I'd been with Cassidy, who had since shipped out. Our sexual play consisted of some fooling around in the showers, and long dinner conversations in Naples in which I tried a number of arguments (all rather weak) to persuade Jimmy Joe to try it out.

Although he'd been sufficiently excited by our shower-room jostling to be willing to hear my arguments, he was afraid that if he did it with me, he'd turn "queer." The whole prospect was really troubling for him. Instead, he was still hoping to be rescued from temptation by some satisfactory experience with women in one of the cities he went to on flights as an on-board mechanic. In the end, that's precisely what happened.

By that time, my duties had expanded to include some flying time as a cargo handler on the DC-3s that delivered stuff to other American bases in Europe (which was the primary mission of the detachment). Although I still worked under Petty Officer First Class Parr's supervision, I was now assigned to the detachment's legal officer, Lieutenant Fitzpatrick, whose duties included the investigation of the outfit's internal affairs.

One night I returned to Naples from a flight that had gone to Port Lyautey, Morocco. Instead of turning in, I headed downtown to a basement nightclub where some of the guys drank—the same one where my "double," Charlie S., had partied with his mates. I no doubt hoped to run into Jimmy Joe. In the smoky, low-ceilinged room that featured a circular bar, I shouldered my way through the crowd and got a scotch and soda. Standing across the bar from me, I noticed, was Parr, well into an evening of hard drinking.

I'd worked for Parr for two years and I don't recall that we'd ever exchanged a word, friendly or otherwise, outside of the office. This was the first time I'd run into him "on shore," though occasionally I'd silently noted the morning-after effects of his nights on the town. He saw me and made his way around the bar until he was at my side. We exchanged a perfunctory greeting.

Parr then said in a dead-sober voice, in a tone as casual as if he were ordering me to fetch a file, "Some kid said something to Chief W—(and here he named the airplane mechanics' chief petty officer), and he went to Fitzpatrick. So you'd better be careful." I knew exactly what he was talking about and so, to my astonishment, did Parr. That was it. No questions. No moral judgments. No commiseration. Just a flat-out warning. Parr then crossed the room to join some men of his own rank.

The next morning, I found Jimmy Joe. "Are you out of your mind?" I asked and drew him off to a quiet corner of the hangar. I found out how far it had gone: Jimmy Joe had gone to his chief for some fatherly advice. It had stayed pretty vague, on the level of, *What should you do if you think someone's coming on to you?* Jimmy had mentioned my name, but made it clear that nothing had happened. After I'd surveyed the damage, I explained to Jimmy in mostly one-syllable words, except for the phrase "conduct unbecoming," what all of it meant and exactly what kind of trouble both of us could get into. He seemed to understand.

I then scampered up the ladder to the upstairs office at the back of the hangar, breezed in, went up to Fitzpatrick as I normally did at the beginning of the day, looked him in the eye, said, "Good morning, Lieutenant. Ready for some coffee, sir?" and awaited his orders. That was that.

Parr never mentioned the incident again. I was indeed more careful, and Lieutenant Fitzpatrick subsequently found no cause to raise the matter with me.

If Parr hadn't warned me, a number of things could easily have happened: getting caught (if not with Jimmy, someone else), getting kicked out (of the navy), getting stuck with a fate worse than death. Instead of inventing "gay liberation" (along with a few hundred thousand others) in 1969, I would have had years of psychiatrists and, after several twelve-step-program failures and decades of closeted self-hatred, would've had to re-come out as a man of thirty-five or forty.

What I don't know is why Parr warned me. I don't know (won't ever know) if Parr was gay and thus had some idea of protecting his own, or if a more complex set of reasons and loyalties motivated his decision to warn me. I only knew—and perhaps that's *all* we can know at certain times—that I had been saved.

Unfriendly

Mette Bach

On MySpace recently, I "friended" a woman named Salty Sam. I'd met her a few times, at bars. She was the rowdy one, the one who made the crowd stop chattering, call her name. She was like Norm from *Cheers*, only female, tattooed, twenty years younger, and way more punk. So she wasn't *like* Norm. There was still something Norm-like about her, a joviality, a quick wit and plenty of friends.

Adding people as friends on MySpace is different from becoming friends in real life. I can't say I'm particularly gifted at either. I rarely walk up to someone and boldly offer a handshake and an introduction. I should but I don't. Or I would but I can't. Or I could but I won't. The point is that even in the real world, I tend to keep to myself. But that particular night, I read her blog and liked how cranky she was. I have a bizarre fondness for online crankiness. I don't care for it in person, but online I like the ranters, the pithy twerps, the debaters, and the cynics. It works for me.

The next day, I logged on to find a message from my new friend. Only she wasn't my friend and her message wasn't what I expected. She asked why on earth she would want to be friends with me and why was I so desperate to have a token dyke friend anyway.

I'm not going to lie. My feelings were hurt. Rationally, I know it's just a stupid website and she probably didn't mean it to sound the way it read in my inbox—but I couldn't help but feel rejected and judged. I immediately apologized for making her feel tokenized and told her that I'd met her some years back through my ex, and inserted a female name, and mentioned seeing her in the bars. I had a strong need to justify my own queerness.

But the more I thought about it, the more I found the whole exchange to be unsatisfactory. Would it be so terrible to be friends with me if I were straight? Does my bedmate really factor that highly in my capacity to be an online friend? And, even if she really is only interested in being friends with other lesbians, why couldn't she take the time to make sure about me? On my MySpace profile, I list *lesbian* as my sexuality, I have mostly queer friends (though, perhaps, like me, they don't look queer enough), I blog about the gay and lesbian bookstore where I work. I don't need a "token dyke friend" because I am a dyke. All she would have had to do was scroll down.

I'll admit I'm sensitive. I try not to be, but I am. I tried to brush off our exchange and after a few days, my hurt feelings subsided and I considered the possibility that she could have been drunk at the time she sent that message, or careless, or maybe she was just mean. But a much more scary interpretation of events was that she was honest. Appearances count and I simply wasn't dykey enough to be accepted into the sisterhood, no questions asked.

Regardless of how queer a life I lead, I'm an invisible member of the community. Even with my sweetheart on my arm, we're just as likely to be mistaken for a nice and friendly—if not somewhat conservative—straight couple. Her in her button-down shirt with a tie to match and her polished boots and sweater jacket, and me in my standard jeans and turtleneck ensemble, don't look like a classic lesbian couple, I'm told. It's made me wonder what, exactly, a lesbian couple looks like. Were I cooler looking, perhaps I'd try a streak of hot pink in my hair, or maybe wear camouflage or army boots. Or maybe there's more to it than fashion.

It's something I don't feel welcome expressing to others. Talking about it is uncomfortable. People tell me I should count myself among the privileged. At least, they say, I'm not a victim of homophobia. At least, I don't receive chilly looks or snide remarks while standing in line at the bank or walking my dogs in the park.

They tell me if I wanted to, I could get a job as an elementary school teacher in a ritzy part of town and no one would even bat an eye. And that's not true for all of us.

I acknowledge my privilege, my relative freedom on the sexuality scale. The problem, however, remains. I'm not truly free until we all are. After all, when I look in the mirror, I know that reflection is (at least in part) what "dyke" looks like.

As for Salty Sam: when she finally accepted me into her entourage of 400 online friends, I was tempted to tell her I respected her initial reaction to my attempt to "friend" her—but I didn't. I just wish I could have gotten into that club without my ex having to vouch for me.

Queer Person First

Tim Miller

In the immense court of my memory ... I come to
meet myself.
—Saint Augustine, *The Confessions*

As someone who has spent his entire adult life writing and performing stories from my "first person" experience, the gnarly terrain of
memoir is both a favorite comfy chair and a particularly scary attic
room. I have bounced between the exquisite pleasures and painful
pitfalls that are inevitably part of the encounter with one's life and
memory. I have put myself (and, of course, my boyfriends) through
the most detailed public revelations of the psychic, emotional, and
sexual autobiographical narratives to which the flesh is heir. I sometimes have to remind myself that not everyone can tolerate their
lives being on display like this. Most people sensibly maintain some
pretty fixed boundaries about what is and is not available for public
consumption. To "rim and tell" loudmouths like me, these boundaries just function as a tempting dare to dive into what I hope might
be a deeper, more naked truth.

I have kept a journal consistently since I was in fifth grade. The
fact that I first picked up a spiral notebook at the age of ten and
began writing daily about what happened to me is every bit as important a detail about who I am as the fact that when I was fourteen
I realized that I was gay, and that it was my fate to love the boy
next door. I would hazard that my need as a young boy-child to
document *my* story was tightly bound up with the inchoate inkling
that I would soon also have to re-write *their* story, the heterosexual

narrative. Long before I began dressing like Oscar Wilde when I was fifteen, the impulse to write my memoir was my first declaration to the world that I was here and before too long would also be queer.

My favorite book during that revelatory Wildean sophomore year of high school was *The Confessions* by Jean-Jacques Rousseau. This should have tipped everyone off right then that I was destined to be a naked performance artist! I suppose I was inspired by Rousseau's urgent need in his *Confessions* to spill all the beans: his obsessive masturbation, his penchant for indecent exposure in public parks, and so on. I learned that as salubrious as it is to spill those garbanzos in the privacy of your own three-ring binder, it's even better to spread them out *à la carte* for all to see. Since the moment I first scribbled feverishly in my gay boy's adolescent journal, that crazed scrawl as panicky as a seismograph after an 8.1 earthquake, I have always seen writing about my life as a fundamental act of knowing myself, of claiming space, and of simple survival. The act of remembering and sharing that memory with others became a crucial way to survive the shit that the world would strew in my path. I figured that if Rousseau's autobiographical ranting could start the French Revolution, my own might at least get me through high school so I could finally find a boyfriend.

Speaking of boyfriends, currently I have been writing a lot about my relationship with my partner Alistair. Since he is from Australia, an antipodal land where people are not "blessed" by US citizenship, for thirteen years we have been dealing with the septic tank of homophobic US immigration rules and regulations that determine how we can make a life together. This boils down to the fact that even after the aforementioned thirteen years together we still can't get married and get Alistair a green card, something a straight couple could do after thirteen minutes. This is quite a challenge on top of negotiating the garden-variety difficulties that any two men have in trying to relate to each other. Since I keep trying to stay true to my crazy notion that I should always write about what is on the front burner in my queer life, I am naturally trying to get down on paper the steak tartare of feelings that this existential bi-national relationship is bringing up. Alistair and I have had to fling ourselves around the globe trying to get papers in order, so that our love for each other could find a place to grow. You can forget luxuries like wall-to-wall carpeting and a room with a view. We just want to be in the same time zone.

This sometimes overwhelming international dilemma has tapped me back into the kind of faith I had as a tortured gay teenager, that if I wrote about the hard stuff in my life, it just might make the situation better. During the rigors of trying to survive as a gay boy in hate-filled America, I had somehow begun to believe that the act of writing honestly about my life might be a way to find the potential to transform it. If truth be told, I think I have never stopped believing this. Telling the stories of my life has always carried the potential for liberation. Maybe the writing cure could now help me get a lock once again on a chaotic situation, the nagging fear that at some point Alistair and I will be forced to leave the country. This can really cut through a lot of writer's block. I'm writing as fast as I can before his visa expires! I have never really lost this trust that the act of writing down my story somehow could alchemically affect how the story might end.

A moment ago, I took a break from writing and stepped outside the house that Alistair and I share in Venice Beach. I decided that it was more important that I should spy on Alistair in his office, a small writing cabana next to our gurgling hot tub. Leaving my office with the computer humming its annoyance at my bad work habits, I made a quick detour to the kitchen for a reduced-fat granola bar (empty calories have been proven crucial to the autobiographical writing process!), and I turned the kitchen light off before sneaking outdoors and down to the ugly powder-blue tile the previous owner of the house put down over his failed grass lawn.

Alistair's face is right behind the window of his writing fort. His mouth tenses as he searches for the right word, the exact association, the accessed feeling for the memoir that he is writing about his childhood in the form of an encyclopedia called *The End of the World Book*. He is probably writing from his own memory about the time when a magpie swooped down on him as a child, or about the first time that he came, or about a father who was so distant that he might as well have not existed. Whatever he is writing about, I can see it wander across his face. I, a literary Peeping Tom, try to see what's going on with him so that I can then snare that moment and drag it kicking and screaming back into the house to write about it. I will do this to try to make sense of my chaotic life and to share what sense I may find there with an unsuspecting reader. This act of writing memoir is how Alistair is also doing his part to solve, for the present at least, our immigration problem. Alistair and I are able to be together in the US because he has a work visa to teach writing, in particular creative nonfiction, at Antioch University in Los Angeles. So this subject is near and dear to me, because the act of writing from our lives is both the practical and the psychic mechanism for Alistair and me to share our lives together!

Peeking (all right, spying) at Alistair—as he types away, finishing his forthcoming book—feels a lot like when I try to look at my own life in order to write about it. I take off my shoes, sneak up on myself very quietly. I don't want to scare myself off. I pull out my machete and start to hack away at the tangled vines that block my view. I make decisions, have attacks of selective memory. Sometimes I am too easy on myself; the next moment I describe some ordinary selfish moment more brutally than it probably deserves.

As I look at Alistair writing away in his hut thousands of miles away from the land where he grew up, how can I hope in my own writing to get at the knotty tendons of how complex our real life is? Every time I try to write down anything from my memory, I am pulling the words out through a shrinking device that makes the feelings and the experience and the joys and the shit seem all vaguely squeezed, like trying to coax the last bit of toothpaste (or KY, for that matter!) out of the tube and onto your trembling toothbrush (or tumescent red-purple cock). Like Pepé Le Pew forever caught in the grasp of a Warner Brothers cartoon laundry wringer, I am in trouble every time I start to write down what has gone on in my life.

How can I describe the fall of even a single hair on Alistair's forehead and hope to get anywhere near the ballpark of how tender and hard we can be with one another? When I write about the experiences and feelings that have come up from being in love with a man from another country while living in a society that puts no value on such relationships, how can I get under the covers with the hurt that such a situation brings up inside me? Lately, I often find myself crying at the drop of a hat whenever I actually allow myself to feel the pain of the fact that my partnership with Alistair is totally negated by my own country's immigration laws, part of the platter of rights every heterosexual takes for granted. (Forget the Niagara Falls of tears in London as I watched the West End production of *The Sound of Music* and the Trapp Family Singers—seven Catholic children just like in Alistair's family—escape the Nazis over the Alps spinning on the stage!) These tears are definitely welcome to this tightly wound WASP, and their salt is quite precious to me. Any arrangement of subjects and verbs I might find to describe this reality may well be insufficient by comparison to the actual wet feeling of the tears, yet I know I must keep trying to find these words, write them, fling them from the stage and the page, or I will go fucking nuts from anger and fear.

When I tell the stories from my life I hope I can be at least a tiny bit as authentic and surprising as those tears that creep down my face when I least expect them, when something reminds me of this situation Alistair and I face. I want those tears to get the page wet and tell their own story of how much joy and hurt there is in loving a man from another land. Pushing beyond my bad writing habits (my Mixmaster metaphors, attraction to puns, and shameless hyperbole, for starters), I want to find the words that might invite you into this place where I live. I write these stories in the hope that someone else just might understand what it has felt like to walk around in my smelly shoes. On a good day I can hold these stories in the palm of my hand, in a clear light, toward you.

I know that the words I squeeze out of the tube and onto the page will never be as true or wet as the messy experiences lived from day to day. There is such a sweet hopelessness in trying to write from your life, a built-in certainty that whatever you cull will not be as layered or true as what you go through in a single day. Inevitably, the act of writing will distill, edit, change, compress, compact, alter, disguise, enhance, and reduce the raw mess of living. But parallel to that is another magic trick at work. As real as those perils are, the writing of memoir can also hone, expose, reveal, connect, and dig up something from inside me that I can use to build a future.

I have a big story to tell right now. It fills my memory. It's a story of how I met a man from another land and how I want to be with him, but my country, which I both love and hate, doesn't allow such things. I need to tell this story or I will go crazy. When I write my story I can howl out the rage I feel both at our medieval government and my own shortcomings as a man and a lover. I can draw attention to the injustice. As I write this story, it becomes a completely necessary act of looking at the past as a means of negotiating a more empowered and grounded relationship in an uncertain future. Each in our own way, Alistair and I are writing our memoirs of what has happened as a way of creating a future together.

I have a completely unsubstantiated faith that if I write this story,

I may be able to affect how the story will end. I have always used the memories of things past to rewrite the ending of what is to come. I have done this from that first moment that I picked up my spiral binder at the edge of ten, and somehow knew that the queer boy star of my story was not going to end up hanging by his neck from a beam in our family's detached suburban garage. I tell these first person stories of who I have been to imagine who I might become. Writing memoir is a fierce act of imagining the future.

The Future of Francis

Ivan E. Coyote

Francis is a little boy who liked to wear dresses when he was three. The middle son of one of my most beloved friends, he is the fearless fairy child who provided me with living, pirouetting proof that gender outlaws are just born like that, even in cabins in the bush with no running water or satellite television. He confirmed my theory that some of us come out of the factory without a box or with parts that don't match the directions that tell our parents how we are supposed to be assembled.

Watching Francis grow up taught me that what makes him and I different was not bred into us by the absence of a father figure or a domineering mother, or being exposed to too many show tunes or power tools at an impressionable stage in our development. We are not hormonal accidents, evolutional mistakes, or created by a God that would later disown us. Most of us learn at a very early age to keep our secret to ourselves, to try to squeeze into clothes that feel like they belong on someone else's body and hope that the mean kids at school don't look at us long enough to find something they need to pound out of us.

But Francis had a mother that let him wear what he wanted, and Francis had evidence that he was not alone, because Francis had me.

He is eleven now, and I got to hang out with him and his brothers last January, up in Dawson City, Yukon. He doesn't wear dresses anymore, and I didn't see much of his younger self in the gangly boy body he is growing into. He is a tough guy now, too cool to hug me when his friends are around, full of wisecracks and small town street smarts. He can ride a unicycle, juggle, and do head spins. He listens to hip-hop and is not afraid to get in a fistfight. He calls other kids faggot, just like his friends do, but only when his mother can't hear him.

I can't help but wonder if the politics of public school have pushed him to conform, or if he has just outgrown his cross-dressing phase and become as butch a son as any father could hope for. I try to imagine what it would be like for him to be the only boy in a dress on a playground full of kids whose parents are trappers and hunters. To be labeled queer in a town of seventeen hundred people and more than its fair share of souls who survived residential schools, families with four generations of inherited memories of same-sex touches that left scars and shame and secrets. I don't blame him for hiding his difference here, for fighting to fit in.

I walk past his school one day on my way to buy groceries, and watch him kick a frozen soccer ball around in the snow with his buddies. He sees me, and stands still for a second, breathing silver clouds of steam into the cold. When he was little he used to fling himself through the front door when I came to visit, and jump on me before I was all the way out of my truck. He would wrap his whole body around my neck and hips and whisper wet secrets and slobber kisses into my ear. Now he barely returns my wave before he turns and disappears into a sea of snowsuits and scarf-covered faces. I find myself searching the crowd for a boy I barely recognize, a Francis who has outgrown my memory of him. I miss the Francis he used to be, the boy-girl who confessed to me when he was five years old that I was his favorite uncle because we were the same kind of different. Now I can't tell him apart from all the other boys wearing blue parkas.

I realize later I am doing to Francis exactly what I wish the whole world would stop doing to our children: wanting him to be something he is not, instead of just allowing him to be exactly what he is.

I don't want Francis to spend his lunch break being tormented and beaten up. I remember growing my hair in junior high and wanting everyone to like me, and I will never forget the blond boy from school who walked like a girl, and that time in eighth grade someone slammed his face against a locker door and gave him a concussion because he wanted to try out for the cheerleading team. By tenth grade he had learned to eat his lunch alone in an empty classroom and wear his gym shorts under his jeans, but everybody acted like they were his best friend after he shot himself in the head with his stepfather's hunting rifle during spring break the year we all graduated. They hung his school photo up in the hallway and all the kids pinned paper flowers and rest in peace notes to the wall around his picture, but nobody wrote that they were sorry for calling him faggot or sticking gum in his hair or making fun of how he threw a ball.

I made a silent promise to Francis the day I left Dawson City, to always love what he is right now as much as I loved who he was back then. Whether he grows up to become a textbook heterosexual he-man or one day rediscovers his early love for ladies' garments, I will always be his favorite uncle, no matter what he's wearing.

About the Authors

Mette Bach is a Danish-born Canadian writer whose syndicated lesbian humor column, "Not That Kind of Girl," appears in queer newspapers in the US and Canada; she has also contributed to *The Globe and Mail, The Vancouver Review, Harrington Lesbian Fiction Quarterly*, and *Ultimate Lesbian Erotica*. She lives in East Vancouver, and is enrolled in the MFA program in Creative Writing at the University of British Columbia.

S. Bear Bergman is an author, theater artist, instigator, gender-jammer, and good example of what happens when you overeducate a contrarian. Ze is also the author of *Butch Is a Noun* (Suspect Thoughts Press, 2006) and three award-winning solo performances, as well as a frequent contributor to anthologies on all manner of topics from the sacred to the extremely profane. Bergman lives on the Web at *sbearbergman.com*, splits hir tax dollars between Northampton, Massachusetts, and Toronto, Ontario, and feels at home in a lot of places.

Kate Bornstein is an author, playwright, and performance artist. Her books include *Gender Outlaw: On Men, Women, and the Rest of Us; My Gender Workbook; Hello, Cruel World: 101 Alternatives to Suicide for Teens, Freaks, and Other Outlaws*; and (in collaboration with Caitlin Sullivan) the cyber-romance-action novel, *Nearly Roadkill*. Her plays and performance pieces include *Strangers in Paradox; Hidden: A Gender; The Opposite Sex is Neither; Virtually Yours*; and *y2kate: gender virus 2000*. Ze lives with hir partner, sex pioneer, writer, and performance artist Barbara Carrellas, in New York City.

sharon bridgforth is the Lambda Award-winning author of *the bull-jean stories* and of *love conjure/blues* (both RedBone Press), a performance/novel that she tours as text installation. Her work has been anthologized and produced widely and has received support from funding sources including The National Endowment for the Arts/Theatre Communications Group Playwright in Residence Program; Rockefeller Foundation Multi-Arts Production Fund Award; and Funding Exchange/The Paul Robeson Fund for Independent Media. bridgforth is the Anchor Artist for The Austin Project, sponsored by The Center for African and African American Studies (University of Texas at Austin) where she teaches a course on Black Empowerment and Community Internships. Contact: *sharonbridgforth.com*.

Ivan E. Coyote was born and raised in Whitehorse, Yukon Territory. A renowned performer and the award-winning author of three story collections and a novel, Ivan's first love is live storytelling; over the last twelve years she has become an audience favorite at music, poetry, spoken word, and writers' festivals from Anchorage to Amsterdam. Ivan is a columnist for *Xtra! West* magazine, writes regularly for *The Georgia Straight* and CBC Radio, and pops up in periodicals all across the continent. Ivan is at work writing a graphic novel with her cousin, artist and illustrator Dan Bushnell, and recording a CD of live stories with music by songwriters Veda Hille, Dan Mangan, and Rae Spoon. Her first novel, *Bow Grip*, was published by Arsenal Pulp Press in 2006.

Joshua Dalton was born in 1989 and attends college in Richardson, Texas. His writing has appeared in *The Full Spectrum: A New Generation of Writing about Gay, Lesbian, Bisexual, Transgender, Questioning, and Other Identities* (Knopf) and *Userlands: New Fiction Writers from the Blogging Underground* (Akashic).

Mary M. Davies grew up in Halifax, Nova Scotia. Her short story "Dead Horses" was published in *Arts & Letters: Journal of Contemporary Culture,* and has since been nominated for a Pushcart Prize. She is co-editor of *Pinned Down by Pronouns* (Conviction Books), which was nominated for a Lambda Literary Award. Her work has also appeared in *Hot & Bothered 4: Short Short Fiction on Lesbian Desire* (Arsenal Pulp Press). Mary is a frequent reader at Gender Crash, an open-mic event founded and hosted by Gunner Scott, and from 2001–05 she wrote a column for *GenderCrash. com* called "Notes from a Comfortable Shoes Femme." She has recently completed her first novel.

Christopher DiRaddo is working on his first novel, tentatively titled *Remission*, which is about a gay boy and his mother. Two of his short stories appeared in *Quickies 3* (Arsenal Pulp Press). He lives and writes in Montreal where he remains the titleholder of Aigle Noir's Mr. Hairy Chest Contest.

David C. Findlay claims to live in a grey area between the USA and the Arctic, stubbornly refusing to choose one or the other. He splits his time among working as an artist/pornographer/educator, playing with technology, and crusading against bi-narism everywhere.

Katherine V. Forrest is the internationally known author of fifteen works of fiction, including the lesbian classic *Curious Wine* and the Kate Delafield mystery series, a three-time winner of the Lambda Literary Award. A recipient of the Lambda Literary Foundation's Pioneer Award, she was senior editor at Naiad Press for ten years and is currently supervising editor at Spinsters Ink. She has edited or co-edited numerous anthologies, and her stories, articles, and reviews have appeared in publications worldwide.

Stacey May Fowles is a writer, text-based visual artist, and a McGill Graduate in English Literature/Women's Studies who has worked in the literary and gallery communities of Montreal, Toronto, and Vancouver. Her written work has been published in various digital and literary publications, including *Fireweed, Kiss Machine,* and *Hive Magazine.* She is a recent recipient of Toronto Arts Council (2004) and Ontario Arts Council (2005) grants for emerging writers, and her first novel, *Be Good,* was published in 2007 by Tightrope Books. She is working on her second novel and a collection of short stories. Contact: *staceymay@staceymayfowles.com.*

R. Gay wears many hats, one of which is that of writer. Her work can be found in *The Best American Erotica 2004,* several editions of *Best Lesbian Erotica, The Mammoth Book of Tales From the Road,* and many others. Contact: *pettyfictions.com.*

Daniel Gawthrop is the author of four nonfiction books, including *Affirmation: The AIDS Odyssey of Dr. Peter* (New Star) and *The Rice Queen Diaries: A Memoir* (Arsenal Pulp Press). He lives in Vancouver, British Columbia.

Sky Gilbert is a writer, director, and drag queen extraordinaire. He was co-founder and artistic director of Buddies in Bad Times Theatre (North America's largest gay and lesbian theater) for eighteen years. He is the author of novels including *Guilty, St. Stephen's, I Am Kasper Klotz,* and *Brother Dumb*; the theater memoir *Ejaculations from the Charm Factory* (ECW); two poetry collections, *Digressions of a Naked Party Girl* and *Temptations for a Juvenile Delinquent* (both ECW); and the play *Bad Acting Teachers* (Playwrights Canada Press). He has received two Dora Mavor Moore Awards and the Pauline McGibbon Award for theater directing, and was recently the recipient of the Margo Bindhardt Award (from the Toronto Arts Foundation), the Silver Ticket Award (from the Toronto Alliance for the Performing Arts), and the ReLit Award for his fourth novel, *An*

English Gentleman (Cormorant Books). He also recently received a PhD from the University of Toronto. Sky holds a University Research Chair in Creative Writing and Theatre Studies at the School of English and Theatre Studies at Guelph University.

Chong-suk Han is the former editor of the *International Examiner*, the oldest continuously publishing pan-Asian Pacific American newspaper in North America. His writings have appeared in more than two dozen different magazines, newspapers, books, and journals. He teaches at Temple University in Philadelphia

Arden Eli Hill is a genderqueer queer writer born and bred in the swamps of Louisiana. He fled to the Boston area for college, then returned south to pursue an MFA in Poetry at Hollins University. He is an assistant poetry editor for *The Hollins Critic* and a poetry editor for *Breath & Shadow*, an online journal of disability and culture.

Nalo Hopkinson, born in Jamaica, has lived in Canada since 1977. She is the author of the novels *The New Moon's Arms, The Salt Roads, Midnight Robber*, and *Brown Girl in the Ring*, as well as the short story collection *Skin Folk* (all Warner Books). She has also edited the anthologies *So Long Been Dreaming: Post-Colonial Science Fiction* (Arsenal Pulp Press), *Mojo: Conjure Stories* (Warner Books), *Whispers from the Cotton Tree Root: Caribbean Fabulist Fiction* (Invisible Cities Press), and *Tesseracts Nine* (Edge).

George K. Ilsley is the author of *Random Acts of Hatred* and *ManBug* (both Arsenal Pulp Press). In 2007, he will be writer in residence at the Berton House Writer's Retreat in the Yukon. His website is *ThatWriter.ca*.

Josh Kilmer-Purcell was raised in rural Wisconsin, and in 1991 graduated from Michigan State University with a BA in English Literature. In 2006, he published the *New York Times* bestselling memoir, *I Am Not Myself These Days* (HarperCollins). He contributes features and pens a popular monthly column for *Out* magazine, and recently completed the screenplay for his memoir, which is being produced by Clive Barker. Kilmer-Purcell and his partner divide their time between their Manhattan apartment and their farm in upstate New York.

Sandra Lambert's writing has appeared in *Conte: A Journal of Narrative Writing* and *Breath and Shadow*, and is also featured in the video project *At the Corner of Me and Myself: Voices of Multicultural Identity*.

Blaine Marchand's poetry and prose has appeared in magazines across Canada and the US. He has won several prizes for his writing, including the Archibald Lampman Award for Poetry for his book *A Garden Enclosed*, and has published a children's novel and three other books of poetry. He has been active in the literary scene for thirty years, having been a co-founder of the *Canadian Review*, *Sparks* magazine, the Ottawa Independent Writers, and the Ottawa Valley Book Festival. He was president of the League of Canadian Poets from 1991–93 and was a monthly columnist for *Capital Xtra!*, Ottawa's gay and lesbian publication, for nine years. His fifth book, *Equilibrium* will be published in 2008. He is Senior Program Manager at the Canadian International Development Agency.

Robin Metcalfe has been a gay activist and journalist for the national and international gay press since the mid-1970s. His fiction, poetry, and essays have been published in four languages on four continents; in more than fifty magazines, including *The Body Politic*, *First Hand*, and *Mandate*; and in many anthologies, including *The Mammoth Book of New Gay Erotica*, *The Second Gates of Paradise*, and the original *Flesh and the Word*. He has worked for twenty years as a critic and curator in the visual arts, and organized the 1997 exhibition *Queer Looking, Queer Acting: Lesbian and Gay Vernacular*. He lives in Halifax, Nova Scotia, where he is Director/Curator of the Saint Mary's University Art Gallery.

Tim Miller is an internationally acclaimed solo performer and has presented his work at such venues as the Yale Repertory Theater, the London Institute of Contemporary Art, the Walker Art Center, Actors Theater of Louisville and the Brooklyn Academy of Music Next Wave Festival. He is the author of the books *Shirts & Skin*, *Body Blows*, and most recently *1001 Beds*, an anthology of his performances and essays. Miller has taught performance at UCLA, NYU, and the Claremont School of Theology. He is a cofounder of two of the most influential performance spaces in the US: Performance Space 122 on Manhattan's Lower East Side, and Highways Performance Space in Santa Monica, California. He website: *hometown. aol.com/millertale*.

Bonnie J. Morris's writing includes the nonfiction books *The Eden Built By Eves: the Culture of Women's Music Festivals* (Alyson) and *Girl Reel: Growing up at the Movies* (Coffee House), the novel *The Question of Sabotage* (Bella), and the story collection *Fifty-two Pickup* (Bella). She has been a finalist for the Frank O'Hara and Judy Grahn Awards, and twice for the Lambda Literary Award. She is an assistant professor in the Women's Studies department at George Washington University.

Achy Obejas is the author of two novels, *Days of Awe* (Ballantine) and *Memory Mambo* (Cleis), both of which won the Lambda Literary Award; the short story collection, *We Came all the Way from Cuba So You Could Dress Like This?* (Cleis); and the poetry collection, *This Is What Happened in Our Other Life* (A Midsummer Night's Press). She is also editor of the anthology *Havana Noir* (Akashic). An accomplished journalist, she worked for the *Chicago Tribune* for more than a decade, and has also written for the *Village Voice*, the *Los Angeles Times*, *Vogue*, *Playboy*, *Ms.*, *The Nation*, *The Advocate*, *Windy City Times*, *High Performance*, *Chicago Sun-Times*, *Chicago Reader*, *Nerve.com*, *Latina*, and *Out*, among others. Among her many honors, she has received a Pulitzer Prize for a *Tribune* team investigation, the Studs Terkel Journalism Prize, and several Peter Lisagor journalism honors, as well as residencies at Yaddo, Ragdale, and the Virginia Center for the Arts. She has served as Springer Writer-in-Residence at the University of Chicago and the Distinguished Writer in Residence at the University of Hawai'i, and is currently the Sor Juana Visiting Writer at DePaul University in Chicago.

Joy Parks began her writing career by lying about her age to the editor of her hometown newspaper. She was a columnist for *The Body Politic*, Canada's infamous (and long defunct) gay newsmagazine, and has written for many GLBT and mainstream publications including *The San Francisco Chronicle*, *The Boston Globe*, *The Toronto Star*, *The Ottawa Citizen*, *The Globe and Mail*, *Gay and Lesbian Review Worldwide*, *The Advocate*, *Lambda Book Report*, *Girlfriends*, and *Publishers Weekly*. "Sacred Ground," her (sometimes) monthly column on lesbian writing, can be found online. She began writing fiction as a fortieth birthday present to herself, and has since published stories in nearly a dozen anthologies, including *The Future is Queer* (Arsenal Pulp Press).

Stan Persky teaches philosophy at Capilano College in North Vancouver, British Columbia. He is the author of several books, including *Then We Take Berlin* (Vintage), *Buddy's: Meditations on Desire, Autobiography of a Tattoo, The Short Version: An ABC Book*, and *Topic Sentence: A Writer's Education* (all New Star), from which his essay is excerpted. He lives in Vancouver and Berlin.

Andy Quan is the author of two collections of short fiction, *Six Positions: Sex Writing* (Green Candy) and *Calendar Boy* (New Star), and the poetry collection *Slant* (Nightwood Editions). He is the co-editor of *Swallowing Clouds* (Arsenal Pulp Press), an anthology of Canadian-Chinese poetry, and has also recorded two albums, *Take-off and Landings* (1999) and *Clean* (2002). More info at *andyquan.com*.

Kirk Read is the author of *How I Learned to Snap* (Penguin), a memoir about being out in high school in Virginia. He has worked as an HIV counselor, phlebotomist, and volunteer coordinator at St James Infirmary, a free health care clinic for sex workers. His forthcoming collection of essays is called *This is the Thing,* and he is in the middle of a novel and a second memoir about sex work. He can be found at *kirkread.com*.

Gayle Roberts is a retired high school teacher in Vancouver, British Columbia, who transitioned "on the job" in 1996. For a number of years, she was the chair of the Zenith Foundation and the treasurer of the Trans Alliance Society, an umbrella group of BC trans organizations and allies. Currently, Gayle is the chair of the Vancouver Coastal Health Authority's Advisory Group to the Trans Health Program. She is a member of Quirk-e, the Queer Imaging and (W)Riting (K)Collective for Elders.

Jeffrey Rotin is a freelance writer, magazine editor, and consultant to non-profit organizations. Born in Toronto, Ontario, he has lived in Vancouver, British Columbia, since 1995.

D. Travers Scott is the author of two novels, the Lambda Literary Award winner *One of These Things Is Not Like the Other* and *Execution, Texas: 1987.* Deemed "funny and disturbing" by David Sedaris and "halfway between Flaubert and *Straight to Hell*" by Robert Glück, Scott's work has appeared in venues such as "This American Life," *Harper's, The Mammoth Book of New Gay Erotica, Switch Hitters: Lesbians Write Gay Male Erotica and Gay Men Write Lesbian Erotica, PoMoSexuals: Challenging*

Assumptions About Gender and Sexuality, and the *Best Gay Erotica* and *Best American Gay Fiction* series. He is pursuing a PhD in Communication at the University of Southern California. More info at *dtraversscott. com.*

Simon Sheppard is the editor of *Homosex: Sixty Years of Gay Erotica,* and the author of *In Deep: Erotic Stories; Kinkorama: Dispatches From the Front Lines of Perversion; Sex Parties 101;* and the award-winning *Hotter Than Hell and Other Stories.* His work has appeared in about 250 anthologies, including many editions of *The Best American Erotica* and many, many of *Best Gay Erotica.* He writes the syndicated column "Sex Talk," the online serial "Dirty Boys Club," and hangs out (wildly) at *simonsheppard.com.*

David Hatfield Sparks is a musician, ethnomusicologist, writer, educator, and librarian. He is the co-author with Randy Connor of the *Encyclopedia of Queer Myth, Symbol, and Spirit* (Cassell) and *Queering Creole Spiritual Traditions* (Haworth). His essay "And Revolution Is Possible: Re-Membering the Vision of This Bridge," also co-authored with Randy, his partner of twenty-eight years, appeared in *This Bridge We Call Home: Radical Visions for Transformation* (Routledge). He recently finished a poetry chapbook entitled *Princes and Pumpkins,* and is completing a new book on queer spirituality, *Wings of Eros: Explorations in Queer Spirit.*

Shawn Syms has written about addiction and recovery for *The Globe and Mail, Spacing,* and *Eye Weekly,* and about sexuality, politics, and culture for many other publications, including *Xtra!, Gay Community News,* and *PWA Coalition Newsline.* He lives in Toronto.

Therese Szymanski has been shortlisted for a Spectrum, a few Lammies and Goldies, and made the Publishing Triangle's list of notable lesbian books. She writes the Brett Higgins Motor City Thrillers (*When the Dancing Stops, When the Dead Speak, When Some Body Disappears, When Evil Changes Face, When the Corpse Lies,* and *When First We Practice*); edited *Back to Basics, Call of the Dark, Wild Nights, Fantasy,* and *A Perfect Valentine,* has novellas in *Once Upon a Dyke, Stake through the Heart,* and *Bell, Book and Dyke*; and has a few dozen published short stories.

Karen Taylor's writing can be seen in *Best Date Ever: True Stories That Celebrate Lesbian Relationships* (Alyson), *Best Lesbian Love Stories:*

NYC Edition (Alyson), *Friday the Rabbi Wore Lace* (Cleis), *Best Trans-gender Erotica* (Circlet), *My Lover, My Friend* (Alyson), *The Academy: Tales of the Marketplace* (Mystic Rose), and others. She has also put her Jewish graduate degree to other creative uses: she developed a leather-oriented Passover haggadah with her spouse, author Laura Antoniou, titled *Avadim Chayinu* (*Once We Were Slaves*). She is currently collaborating with Antoniou on *Slaves of the Marketplace*, a short story collection set in Antoniou's infamous Marketplace series. She works full time as the director of an LGBT senior center in Queens, New York.

Jason Timermanis lives in Toronto, and is at work on his first novel.

Jane Van Ingen is a manager at a nonprofit in NYC that supports people with disabilities as they search for employment. A former journalist, her book reviews, articles and poetry have appeared in *Lambda Book Report, Gay City News, New York Blade, Poets & Writers,* and *East Village,* and on *Poetz.com.*

Gregory Woods is a poet, literary critic, and teacher. His poetry collections are *We Have the Melon* (1992), *May I Say Nothing* (1998), *The District Commissioner's Dreams* (2002), and *Quidnunc* (2007), all from Carcanet Press. His critical works include *Articulate Flesh: Male Homo-eroticism and Modern Poetry* (1987) and *A History of Gay Literature: The Male Tradition* (1998), both from Yale University Press. He is professor of gay and lesbian studies at Nottingham Trent University, England.

About the Editors

Richard Labonté writes book reviews, edits books, translates technical writing into real English, and reads a lot. He founded and worked with A Different Light Bookstores from 1979 to 2000, and edits anthologies for Cleis Press, including the *Best Gay Erotica* series, *Hot Gay Erotica*, *Country Boys*, *Where the Boys Are*, *Best Gay Romance 2008*, *Best Gay Bondage*, and *Boys in Heat: Gay Erotic Stories*. He has also co-edited *The Future is Queer* (Arsenal Pulp Press) with Lawrence Schimel. His favorite workspaces are the porch of a 200-acre farm in Calabogie, Ontario, co-owned with several college friends for more than thirty years, or the deck of a home on Bowen Island, a short ferry ride from Vancouver, British Columbia, owned by one of those college friends; he lives in both places with his husband Asa. Contact: *tattyhill@gmail.com*.

Lawrence Schimel is a full-time author and anthologist who's published over eighty books, including *The Future is Queer* (with Richard Labonté; Arsenal Pulp Press); *Best Date Ever: True Stories That Celebrate Gay Relationships* (Alyson); *Two Boys in Love* (Seventh Window); *The Drag Queen of Elfland* (Circlet); *The Mammoth Book of New Gay Erotica* (Carroll & Graf); *Fairy Tales for Writers* (A Midsummer Night's Press); and *Vacation in Ibiza* (NBM); among others. His *PoMoSexuals: Challenging Assumptions About Gender and Sexuality* (with Carol Queen; Cleis) won a 1998 Lambda Literary Award; and he has also been a finalist for the Lambda Literary Award ten other times. The German edition of his anthology *Switch Hitters: Lesbians Write Gay Male Erotica and Gay Men Write Lesbian Erotica* (with Carol Queen; Cleis) won the Siegesseuele Best Book of the Year Award. He won the 2002 Rhysling Award for Poetry. His children's book *No hay nada como el original* (Destino) was selected by the International Youth Library in Munich for the 2005 White Ravens award and his children's book *¿Lees un libro conmigo?* (Destino) was selected by the 2007 International Board of Books for Young People as an Outstanding Books for Young People with Disabilities. His work has been anthologized in *The Random House Book of Science Fiction Stories*; *Best of Best Gay Erotica*; *Gay Love Poetry*; *The Sandman: The Book of Dreams*, *Chicken Soup for the Horse-Lover's Soul 2*; and *The Random House Treasury of Light Verse*, among many others. He has also contributed to numerous periodicals, from *The Christian Science Monitor* to *Physics Today* to *Gay Times*. His writings have been translated into over twenty languages. For two years he served as co-chair of the Publishing Triangle, and for five years he served as the Regional Advisor of the Spain Chapter of the Society of Children's Book Writers and Illustrators. Born in New York City in 1971, he currently lives in Madrid, Spain with his husband, Ismael Attrache.